Aligning Mind and Heart

Aligning Mind and Heart

Leadership and Organization Dynamics for Advancing K–12 Education

Chris Heasley
Robert Palestini

ROWMAN & LITTLEFIELD
Lanham • Boulder • New York • London

Published by Rowman & Littlefield
An imprint of The Rowman & Littlefield Publishing Group, Inc.
4501 Forbes Boulevard, Suite 200, Lanham, Maryland 20706
www.rowman.com

86-90 Paul Street, London EC2A 4NE, United Kingdom

Copyright © 2022 by Chris Heasley and Robert Palestini

All rights reserved. No part of this book may be reproduced in any form or by any electronic or mechanical means, including information storage and retrieval systems, without written permission from the publisher, except by a reviewer who may quote passages in a review.

British Library Cataloguing in Publication Information Available

Library of Congress Cataloging-in-Publication Data

Names: Heasley, Chris, 1977– author. | Palestini, Robert H., author.
Title: Aligning mind and heart : leadership and organization dynamics for advancing K–12 education / Chris Heasley, Robert Palestini.
Description: Lanham, Maryland : Rowman & Littlefield, 2022. | Includes bibliographical references. | Summary: "This book is a go-to guide for school leadership"—Provided by publisher.
Identifiers: LCCN 2021033722 (print) | LCCN 2021033723 (ebook) | ISBN 9781475861402 (cloth) | ISBN 9781475861419 (paperback) | ISBN 9781475861426 (epub)
Subjects: LCSH: Educational leadership. | School management and organization. | Educational planning.
Classification: LCC LB2806 .H4155 2022 (print) | LCC LB2806 (ebook) | DDC 371.2/011—dc23
LC record available at https://lccn.loc.gov/2021033722
LC ebook record available at https://lccn.loc.gov/2021033723

For Kristin, Addison, Cadence, and Rylan. Thank you for loving me, believing in me, supporting me, and pushing me to be a better person every day.

Contents

Acknowledgments	ix
Introduction	1
1 Understanding Organization Structure	3
2 Developing Organization Culture	9
3 Transformative Leadership Models	21
4 Motivation for Change	35
5 Relevance of Communication	45
6 Decision-making Process	55
7 Conflict Management Process	67
8 Empowerment for Success	75
9 Comprehensive and Strategic Planning Models	89
10 Leadership through Change	99
11 Leading with Heart	113
12 What Have We Learned?	121
Appendix: Heart Smart Surveys I and II	127
References	139
Index	143
About the Authors	145

Acknowledgments

A sincere thank you to Tom Koerner, whose continued support in our authorship is much appreciated. We also wish to recognize Carlie Wall for her efforts in helping this book become a reality. Lastly to our department colleagues, we thank you all for being a part of our *think tank* discussions. Much of the content found within these pages came from those conversations.

Introduction

The chapters of this book list vital components of different organizational units (such as faculty departments, educational institutions, and school districts). These topics speak to the so-called science of leadership, but do not necessarily relate to the art of administration and leadership. Still, we remain ever mindful that one needs to lead with both mind (science) and heart (art) to be truly effective. We contend the effective building blocks of quality leadership are the skills of communication, motivation, organizational development, management, and creativity. Mastering the theory and practice in these areas of study will produce high-quality leadership ability and, in turn, produce successful leaders; doing so with "heart" or compassion will result in not only highly successful leadership but what author and scholar Chris Lowney calls "heroic leadership." Figure 1.1 depicts the ten assessments that, when applied in an integrated fashion and with heart, complete a model for effective educational administration.

But how exactly do these assessments work in tandem to ensure successful praxis? Suppose you are standing in the middle of a dense forest. You are asked to describe the characteristics of the forest: What types of trees are growing there? Where are the trees thriving? Where are they not? Faced with this proposition, most people "would not be able to see the forest for the trees." Newly appointed, and not so newly appointed, administrators often have these same feelings of confusion when faced with the prospect of having to assume a leadership role in a complex organization like a department team, school, or a school system/district. Where does one start? An effective way to start would be to systematically examine the components that comprise an organization. Such a process of organizational diagnosis and prescription leads to a comprehensive and integrated analysis of the organization's strengths and weaknesses and points the way toward improvement. This book suggests such a sequential and systematic approach by intentionally giving focus to the "trees" and the "forest." Found at the end of each chapter is a case study. Readers should approach these activities with contemplative mindfulness as they determine a diagnosis (an explanation for the reasons for, or causes of, the behaviors and attitudes described in the case) and envision a prescription (an identified pathway or course of action for particular circumstances based on the foregoing diagnosis). Utilizing this learning strategy can effectively produce dramatic results toward leadership development.

Importantly, each chapter of this book is dedicated to one of the ten essential components of an organization. Most of each chapter focuses on the implementation of these components, but there is some emphasis on the supporting theory that speaks to *why* these leadership practices are effective. We know that leaders are busy people; therefore, we invite our readership to reflect on the brief case study found at the end of each chapter, allowing for one to more deeply consider implications of practice. There is also a *diagnostic debrief*, a list of questions aimed at helping to *quickly* assess the status of these components in your educational organization and whether they need to be addressed. In the Appendices, there are two diagnostic instruments: Heart Smart Surveys I and II that will help quantify the assessment process. If the reader is interested in exploring these topics as applied in a higher education arena, we would suggest reading its complimentary sibling text entitled *Me, Mind, and Heart: Authentic Leadership for Advancing Higher Education* (Heasley and Palestini, 2021). Hopefully, addressing these questions in a systematic and concrete way will enable us to see *both* the forest and the trees and lead our institutions to new heights (pun intended).

Chapter 1

Understanding Organization Structure

> *The master in the art of living makes little distinction between his work and his play, his labor and his leisure, his mind and his body, his education and his recreation, his love and his religion. He hardly knows which is which. He simply pursues his vision of excellence in whatever he does, leaving others to decide whether he is working or playing. To him, he is always doing both.*
>
> —Zen Buddhist text

Educational entities are essentially organized according to one of three basic structures: the classical structure, the social systems structure, or the open-systems structure. Despite being organized around one of these structures, most schools and school systems reflect certain aspects of each of these models (DePree, 1989). These structures are illustrated in figure 1.1.

THE CLASSICAL THEORY

Classical theorists believe that an application of a bureaucratic structure and process will promote rational, efficient, and disciplined behavior, making possible the achievement of well-defined goals. Efficiency, then, is achieved by arranging positions and jurisdiction and by placing power at the top of a clear chain of command. The conceptual model of the classical theory has had a significant impact on education. Virtually every school and school system in the United States is organized according to the tenets of the classical theory.

Within the classical theory framework, the individual is conceived of as an object, a part of the bureaucratic machine. This is the antithesis of the second organizational theory, the social systems theory. Historically,

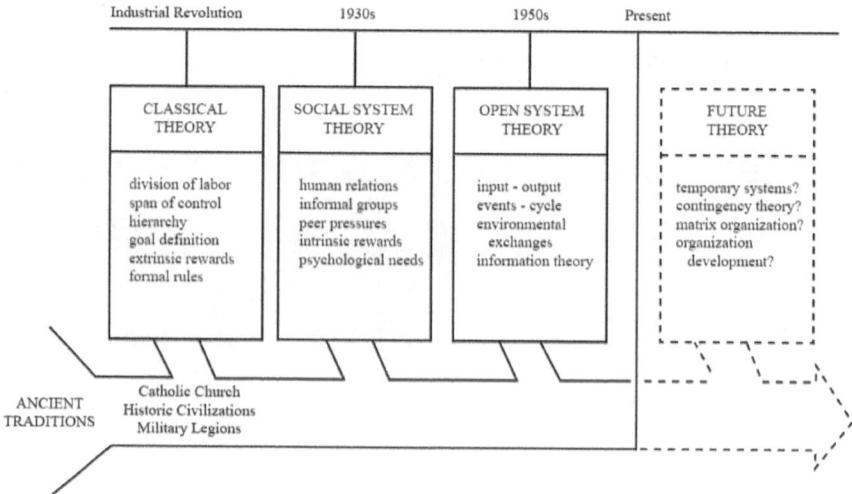

Figure 1.1   Organization Theory and Structures.

researchers found that the impact of social-psychological variables within the worker group was significant. The study of behavior in social system settings intensified, and a greater sophistication developed about how and why group members behave as they do under given conditions. In time a natural social systems orientation to the analysis of behavior evolved in the literature as an alternative to the rational or classical systems approach.

THE SOCIAL THEORY

The conceptual perspective of the social systems model suggests that an organization consists of a collection of groups (social systems) that collaborate to achieve system goals. Coalitions among subgroups within the organization (e.g., English teachers, history teachers, foreign languages teachers) form to provide power bases upon which positive or negative action can be taken (e.g., "Let's all vote to reject writing behavioral objectives."). As with the classical organizational theory, schools and school systems have been profoundly influenced by the social systems model.

THE OPEN SYSTEM THEORY

A newer theory that is having a growing influence on educational institutions, especially higher education institutions, is the open system model.

The classical and social system theories tend to view organizational life as a closed system: that is, as isolated from the surrounding environment. By contrast, open system theory conceives of an organization as a set of interrelated parts that interact with the internal and external environments.

As an ecology-focused model, open system theory receives "inputs" such as human and material resources, values, community expectations, and societal demands; transforms them through a production process (e.g., an educational program); and exports the product in the form of "outputs" (e.g., graduates, new knowledge, revised value sets) into the environment (e.g., businesses, the military, service providers) with "value added." The organization receives a return (e.g., community financial support in the form of taxes or tuition) for its efforts so it can survive and prosper. Then the cycle begins once again. Figure 1.2 illustrates the open system dynamic.

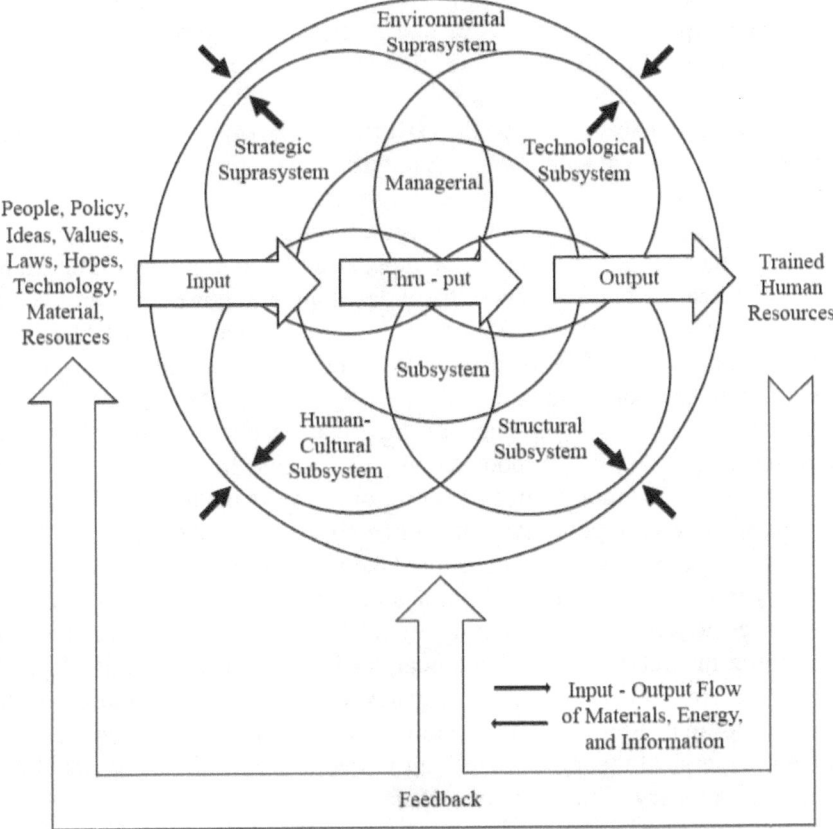

Figure 1.2 Open System Model.

Through the perspective of open system theory, a new logic on issues of organizational governance has emerged. It emphasizes the relationship of the organization to its surrounding environment and, thus, places a premium on planning and programming for events that cannot be controlled directly. The key to making an open system work effectively and efficiently is its ability to gather, process, and utilize information. In an educational institution, then, the facility with which a need is discovered, a goal is established, and resources are coalesced to meet that need will determine the effectiveness and efficiency of that institution. Unlike businesses, educational institutions, especially colleges and universities, have not yet found a way to meet the demands of the open system model.

CONTINGENCY THEORY

In more recent years, a view of organization development has surfaced that treats each organization, and even the entities within the organization, as relatively unique. For centuries, this orientation has been at the core of practitioner behavior, but has been seen basically as an anomaly, reflective of inefficiency or unpreparedness, and thus overlooked by management scientists. Currently, the changing situational character of management is coming to be understood as a key to the management process itself.

Many management scholars and practitioners agree with the observation that contingency theory is perhaps the most powerful current and future trend in the organization field. At this stage of development, however, contingency theory is not really a theory. Rather, it is a conceptual tool that facilitates understanding of the situational flow of events and alternate organizational and individual responses to that flow.

As a conceptual tool, contingency theory does not possess the holistic character of the three major models discussed earlier. In many ways, contingency theory can be thought of as a subset of open system theory because it is through open system theory that one comes to understand the dynamic flows of events, personnel, and resources that take place in organizations.

At any rate, the implication of contingency theory is that in order to have a maximal effective organization structure, institutions should employ the best of all three theoretical models: classical, social, and open systems, depending on the situation. Thus, a contingency organizational structure can be described as an institutional *mindset* rather that an organizational chart, since, unlike the classical theory, it is difficult to depict the attributes of social and open-system theory in the form of a chart.

As a preview of coming attractions, this book will incorporate contingency theory thinking in discussions of leadership, employee motivation, communication, decision-making, conflict resolution, and many other components of an organization.

IMPLICATIONS FOR PRACTICE: UNDERSTANDING ORGANIZATION STRUCTURES CASE STUDY

Bueno Vista, Arizona, is a small urban city with a population of 33,000. The Bueno Vista School District is made up of four elementary schools (K–5), three middle schools (6–8), and two high schools with grades nine through twelve. Despite a violation of a classical organization structure, many of the administrators play dual roles based on a lack of proper resources and funding. The city is divided between two starkly different socioeconomic halves. As a result, half of the district schools are comprised of students from the affluent side of the city and the other schools receive most of the students from communities with less affluence. This causes much competition between the schools in terms of academic rigor, athletic prominence, and learning resources.

The board of education consists of nine members, who serve terms of three years with a turnover of two to three people per year. For many years, the school district did not have a good reputation. The students were known to be unruly, and there was low teacher morale. It was not until a few years ago, when the district hired a superintendent from outside the district, that the reputation began to improve.

Despite favorable regard on account of more structure and an improved management system, the larger Bueno Vista community recently voted against approval of next year's school budget. An article featured the budget defeat, along with other state school districts where the budgets did not pass. Bueno Vista Superintendent was quoted as accepting blame for the budget defeat, stating "[The defeat] suggests I was unable to adequately articulate the reasons for the requested increase in funding." The article further cited school taxes were rising, and the communities felt that they were high enough.

A negative vote was foreseeable. When asked, many people who commented said they voted no because they did not have children in the schools or that their children were grown and out of school. The community did not feel it necessary to take on the extra tax burdens if they did not have children in public schools. Another reason for the budget not passing could also have been the recurring low voter turnout. The people who felt strongly enough about the extra tax got out to vote, but the parents of the children in the schools in favor of the budget failed to do so. This relates back to the division of the community and the problems that often arising because of it.

As a result of the budget defeat, greatly needed and anticipated requests for restructuring were denied. District administrators remained overburdened and school leaders were asked to take on additional tasks and oversight for their learning communities with no additional pay or resources. Additionally, four elementary teaching positions, six non-tenured middle school teachers' jobs, and two high school administrator positions were eliminated.

Programs, in addition to requests for staffing needs, were also negatively impacted by the denied budget vote. Academic and bridge programs were also reviewed to be cut. For instance, the elementary schools had a partially grant-funded developmental first grade program. This class was developed for children who were not only ready for first grade but who were also not candidates for retention in kindergarten. This was a pilot program that could not be funded for another year. The extracurricular sports' teams were also being reviewed. Many teams with low participation were in jeopardy of being cut.

DIAGNOSTIC DEBRIEF

Here are some questions to consider when assessing an institution's organizational structure:

- Are the best aspects of the classical, social systems, and open-systems organizational structures present?
- Is there appropriate division of labor and is it flexible?
- Is the division of labor conducive to reaching organizational goals?
- Is the structure of the organization well designed?
- Is there a respect for human dignity in the organization?
- Do work groups operate effectively and in tandem?
- Does the organization's structure respond to the environmental contingencies?

Chapter 2

Developing Organization Culture

Culture consists of the unwritten laws impressed on the souls of those living under the same constitution.

—*Philo*

When observing a successful salesperson it quickly becomes obvious that much success is based on familiarization of the territory they service. Likewise, organization culture should be a priority for any educational leader. The astute administrator will take a page from *The Music Man's*, Professor Harold Hill, and get to know the territory in their educational institution. Knowing the landscape in education translates into being keenly aware of the organization structure and culture of the institution.

Knowing how one's educational entity is structured within the context of the three models described in chapter 1 is the first step in an educational leader's quest to truly "know the territory." The second step is to be aware of the organization behavior or culture of the institution. Organization culture is composed of the shared beliefs, expectations, values, and norms of conduct of its members. In any organization, the informal culture interacts with the formal structure and control system to produce a generally clear understanding of the "way things are done around here." Even more than the forces of bureaucracy, the organization's culture is the glue that binds people together.

Anyone who has visited a number of educational institutions develops a sense of their different "personalities" or culture. Walking the hallways and campus of an educational institution, a keen observer can see physical manifestations of an underlying set of values: perhaps a huge trophy case in the entrance lobby, classroom desks bolted to the floor, clean and well-maintained grounds, an over-sized football stadium and band programs that overshadow math and science curriculum, faculty and staff constantly patrolling the halls, clandestine meetings of students or faculty, and so forth. Based on a myriad of external observations, institutions have been alternately characterized as union schools, football factories, diploma mills, Blue Ribbon schools, schools of excellence, and learning organizations.

The aforementioned are tangible aspects of the school's culture. The intangible aspects often parallel those values. Schools attempting to develop shared values and enculturate them are often illustrated by symbols frequently found around the schoolyard: "Knowledge is Power"; "Wildcat Pride"; "Education is About Alternatives"; "Not Yet Mindset"; and "All Children Achieving." Other symbols of the school's culture are the heroes and storytellers, faculty members, and/or administrators that have earned legendary status.

Administrators can influence the institution's culture in a positive way. First, however, they must be aware of its importance and its components. If the educational leader has a thorough knowledge of the institution's culture, he or she can set about trying to influence it. One way of doing so is to take time each day to review this and the nine other "secrets" to effective school management that are presented in this book. Ultimately, the best way to influence the institution's culture is by modeling desired behavior. If the leaders want the faculty and staff to be efficient and effective, the leaders need to manifest those same characteristics in their own behavior. However, none of these desired changes will occur unless a culture of mutual trust and respect has been established.

The Processes of Organization Culture

Next, begins an exploration of areas of organization culture that deal with the way leaders perceive events or other people, the way they understand the events and people they perceive, the way past experiences and acquisition of knowledge and information influence this description and diagnosis, and the way leaders form attitudes about the situations based on their perceptions, understanding, and experience. These four processes are referred to as perception, attribution, learning, and attitude formation. Understanding them greatly enhances an administrator's ability to influence the school's culture.

Perception

Perception is the process by which each person senses reality and comes to a particular understanding or view. It is an active process that results in different people having somewhat different, even contradictory, views or understandings of the same event or person. Rarely do different observers describe events or persons in exactly the same way. Often, administrators and their subordinates, coworkers, or supervisors see and describe the same situation differently.

Perceptual Distortions

Perceptions sometimes suffer from inaccuracies or distortions. Although such biases are normal and human, they can have significant consequences when administrators or other members of the institution base action upon potentially invalid distortions. This chapter discusses stereotyping, the halo effect, projection, and the self-fulfilling prophecy as examples. Additional distortions include suppression, repression, denial, displacement, and rationalization (Brodsky, 1988).

Stereotyping

Stereotyping occurs when an individual attributes behaviors or attitudes to a person on the basis of the group or category to which that person belongs. "Low income students aren't as smart as affluent students" and "Principals are all dictators" illustrate stereotyping. Frequently, stereotypes are based on social identity categorizations such as ethnicity, socioeconomic status, gender, and so on, or positions of power (e.g., administrators, faculty, support personnel).

Why does stereotyping occur? Often individuals do not gather sufficient data about others to describe their behaviors or attitudes accurately. They may look for shortcuts to describe certain phenomenon without spending the time to analyze them completely. Alternatively, some individuals have personal biases (both explicit and implicit) against certain groups of individuals (later in this chapter this will be covered more at depth). Historical attitudes toward certain cultural groups may result in stereotypes. Americans may have certain views of Europeans and different views of Japanese, based on their historical experiences with the two groups. Using stereotypes reduces the accuracy of perceptions about these groups.

The Halo Effect

The halo effect refers to an individual letting one salient feature of a person dominate the evaluation of that individual. Being willing to volunteer for extra projects, for example, can cause an administrator to evaluate a teacher as highly competent in the classroom. A neat personal appearance can cause a person to be judged as precise in his or her work and very well organized.

The halo effect frequently occurs in assessments of teacher performance. Individuals may be judged on the basis of one trait, for example, promptness, neatness, or enthusiasm, rather than on a composite of traits and skills over a period of time (Heilmand and Stopeck, 1985).

Projection

One may relate to having heard a teacher say, "My principal is prejudiced; my supervisor is just intimidated by a strong woman" or "my superintendent doesn't like people from marginalized communities!" These observations about these administrators may be accurate, but they may also reflect the teachers' prejudices. Or consider the principal who hesitantly approaches a prospective student's parent, feeling that the parent will not think that the school will offer a quality education to the child. The principal may be seeing his or her own attitudes or feelings about the school in the parent's response, whether or not the parent really feels that way.

Projection refers to an individual's attributing his or her own attitudes or feelings to another person. Individuals use projection as a defense mechanism, to transfer blame to another person, or to provide protection from their own unacceptable feelings. Individuals frequently attribute their own prejudices against members of marginalized communities, supervisors, or employees, for example, to the other party. Hence, projection and its dysfunctional consequences can increase as the work force becomes more diverse; individuals who lack understanding or mistrust people who are different from themselves may project these insecurities onto others.

Self-Fulfilling Prophecy

In many situations, the individuals expect certain behaviors from other individuals or groups. They then see these behaviors as occurring whether or not they actually do. Their expectations become self-fulfilling prophecies. They may expect workers to be lazy, bossy, or tardy; then they perceive they actually are lazy, bossy, or tardy. These expectations may be associated with stereotyping, the halo effect, or projection.

Perceptions of others can be influenced by bias and inaccurate assumptions. Such perceptions have been shown to influence the performance of those for which expectations exists. There is familiarity with the many studies that have linked teacher expectations and student achievement. If a teacher expects a minority student to fail, oftentimes the student does fail. Whereas, if a teacher expects all children to achieve, the children usually achieve. Likewise, if teachers think that their school is going to close as part of a district reorganization plan, the self-fulfilling prophecy oftentimes takes effect and teachers' morale and performance decline and the school actually ends up closing.

DEALING WITH DISTORTIONS

How can dysfunctional perceptual distortions in organizations be reduced?

- First, individuals must gather sufficient information about other people's behavior and attitudes to encourage more realistic perceptions. Administrators, for example, must judge an individual's performance on their observed behavior, rather than on the behavior of a group to which the person belongs.
- Second, administrators must check conclusions they draw to ensure their validity. This includes being aware of explicit and implicit biases (these terms are explained later in this chapter).
- Third, members of the organization must differentiate between facts and assumptions in determining the basis of their perceptions. This work has no end and ought to be omnipresent in the workplace.
- Fourth, individuals must distinguish among various aspects of an individual's behavior, rather than grouping even superficially related aspects. More specifically, they must separate appearance from performance, productivity from attendance, personality from creativity.
- Fifth, to eliminate or reduce projection, individuals must first identify their true feelings. Do they feel anger, uncertainty, and mistrust? After recognizing these feelings, administrators must repeatedly assess whether and how they are influencing their perceptions of others.

THE ATTRIBUTION PROCESS

The need to determine why events occur is common and is inherent in the diagnostic approach that good administrators often take toward problem-solving. Whether consciously or not, it seems most prudent to first ponder the reasons for many events and then decide why the events occurred. In this way, one attributes cause to the events. This process leads to a movement from description to diagnosis. As might be expected, different people often attribute a different cause to the same event.

Attribution theorists and researchers have studied the process of determining the causes of specific events, the responsibility for particular outcomes, and the personal qualities of individuals participating in the situation. For example, some school leaders might deduce the introduction of a new curriculum as the major explanation for a decline in a teacher's performance; if so, situational factors will be attributed for their decline. If, on the other hand, laziness or ineptitude is deemed as influential to their performance, then a leader is likely to conclude that personal dispositions caused the change.

Although both situational and personal factors may have influenced the change in performance, leadership often simplifies understanding and attends primarily to only one cause.

ATTRIBUTION AND LOCUS OF CONTROL

Attribution and the concept of locus of control are closely related. Locus of control is the feeling an individual has about whether they are in control of they own destiny. Whether one believes that internal or external factors affect future events determines whether one has an internal or external locus of control. Those with an internal locus of control believe that future events are determined by their own individual abilities and personal qualities, while those with an external locus of control attribute future outcomes to factors outside of their control.

Thus, the student who attributes a poor performance in a test to the teacher's inability to get the subject across can be said have an external locus of control, while the student who attributes the poor performance to his or her own lack of preparation would tend to have an internal locus of control. The objective, then, for school administrators would be to develop a strong internal locus of control in both themselves and their staffs (Kelley, 1967).

THE LEARNING PROCESS

In addition to perception and attribution, learning—which refers to the acquisition of skills, knowledge, ability, or attitudes—influences the organizational culture of an educational institution. The section that follows focuses on the way individuals learn, beginning with three models of learning and concluding with the administrative implications of learning.

The Behaviorist Approach

Behaviorists emphasize external influences and the power of rewards in learning. They emphasize the link between a given stimulus and response. Recall Pavlov's ground-breaking work with canines. He noted that, upon presentation of powdered meat blown through a tube (unconditioned stimulus) to a dog, the dog salivated (unconditioned response). The ringing of a bell (neutral stimulus) yielded no salivation responses. After pairing the ringing bell with the piece of meat several times, Pavlov then rang the bell without the meat, and the dog salivated (conditioned response). In classical conditioning, after repeated pairing of neutral and unconditioned stimuli, solitary presentation of the neutral stimulus led to a conditioned response (Pavlov, 1927).

Operant conditioning extends classical conditioning to focus on the consequences of a behavior. While a stimulus can still cue a response behavior, the desired or undesired consequence that follows the behavior determines whether the behavior will recur. For example, an individual who receives a bonus (a positive consequence) after creative performance (behavior) on a work assignment (stimulus) is more likely to repeat the creative behavior than if his or her performance is ignored (a negative consequence).

The Cognitive Approach

In contrast to the behavior-reinforcement links that are central to behaviorist theories, cognitive theorists emphasize the internal mental processes involved in gaining new insights. They view learning as occurring from the joining of various cues in the environment into a mental map. In early cognitive experiments, rats learned to run through a maze to reach a goal of food. Repeated trials would cause a rat to develop and strengthen cognitive connections that identified the correct path to the goal (Tolman, 1932).

Employees, too, can develop a cognitive map that shows the path to a specific goal. In this case, the cognitive processes join the stimulus to result in a given behavior. On-the-job training, like a new teacher induction process, should result in a new cognitive map of job performance for junior teachers.

The Social Learning Approach

Extending beyond both behavioral and cognitive learning theories, social learning theory integrates the behaviorist and cognitive approaches with the idea of modeling or imitating behaviors. Learners first watch others who act as models, next develop a mental picture of the behavior and its consequences, and finally try the behavior. If positive consequences result, the learner repeats the behavior; if negative consequences occur, no repetition occurs.

The learning impact occurs when the subject tries the behavior and experiences a favorable result, as in the behaviorist approach. At the same time, the learner's development of a cognitive image of the situation incorporates a basic aspect of cognitive learning. The existence of social learning makes it important that teachers take their responsibility of acting as exemplars for the students very seriously. In addition, administrators need to model the behavior that they expect of the faculty (Bandura, 1978).

IMPLICIT AND EXPLICIT BIAS

Everyone has biases, or preconceived notions made about others. And it is worth confirming there is a myriad of bias types and each may elicit a positive or negative thought or response. Of particular interest is whether one is aware of such thoughts and how they respond or act based on them.

Explicit bias describes the conscious attitudes and beliefs held relevant to a person or group. In some cases, such biases and their expression may arise as the direct result of a perceived threat. Implicit or unconscious bias operates outside of the person's awareness. Interestingly, for some people, implicit bias may be contradictory to their espoused beliefs and values. Unconscious bias can also lead to unintended consequences. Functioning like an auto-correcting text feature, implicit bias can automatically and without full awareness of the person, influence their affect or behavior. Implicit bias can be subcategorized into several types, such as gender bias, racial bias, conformity bias, halo effect, and so on.

CULTURAL COMPETENCY IN THE LEARNING SPACE

There are multiple models, theories, and assessments that seek to illustrate, explain, and measure cultural competency. Simplistically, cultural competency is the ability to understand and effectively communicate across categories of cultural difference. Examples of cultural competency might include a teacher speaking to the negative influence of settler colonialism toward white centeredness, or inclusion of books that positively illustrate children being raised by same-sex parents, or developing curriculum using a variety of textbooks written by both white and nonwhite authors.

Being culturally competent extends beyond attending a one-time professional development experience or being friends with those different than yourself. Conceptually, having a competency of cultural relevance is a constant exercise in understanding and honoring difference. Exposure to varied histories, cultures, languages, traditions, and religious practices are all components that impact one's level of competency.

Being valued matters. Acknowledging individual differences, capacities, and abilities by showing respect, humility, kindness, and curiosity for learning help increase cultural competency awareness and skill development for both school leaders and among students. Current scholars further posit that leaders with high cultural competency demonstrate culturally responsive practices. Such practices recognize and incorporate the skills, assets, and strengths of all members of the organization. Policies, procedures, and practices of a culturally responsive educational organization ensure that learning experiences remain relevant to all students and learning outcomes, instruction, and assessment are aligned to safeguard against exclusionary practices.

MANAGERIAL IMPLICATIONS OF LEARNING

How can school administrators encourage their own and others' learning in the workplace? They can ensure that appropriate conditions for learning exist; providing appropriate stimuli (e.g., professional development materials) should facilitate acquisition of the skills or attitudes desired. Administrators should reinforce desired learned behaviors. They should also provide environmental cues that encourage learning; structuring a context that supports learning is essential. In effect, just as leaders advise teachers to adapt their teaching styles to the variety of learning styles of their students, administrators must adapt their management styles to the variety of learning styles that are present among their faculties.

Administrators can use a modeling strategy for success. For instance, an administrator could identify the goal or target behaviors that will lead to improved performance. After selecting the appropriate model, the administrator must determine whether to present the model through a live demonstration, videotape, other media, or a combination of all of these. Next, the administrator would ensure teachers are capable of meeting the technical skill requirements of the target behavior. As a result of the new learned skill, a more extensive use of cooperative learning activities might lead to improving students' social skills.

If in the aforementioned scenario further change is deemed necessary, the administrator must structure a favorable and positive learning environment to increase the likelihood that the teachers will learn the new behavior and act in the desired way. Starting cooperative learning with a particularly skilled teacher and a cooperative group of students will ensure success. Administrators must also model the target behavior and carry out supporting activities, such as role playing. Conducting a faculty meeting using cooperative learning techniques would be an example of such a strategy.

Continued practice warrants continued success. Administrators should positively reinforce reproduction of the target behaviors both in training and in the workplace. Teacher-of-month awards are an example of this strategy.

Once the target behaviors are reproduced, administrators must maintain and strengthen them through a system of rewards until the behavior is institutionalized; that is, it becomes part of the school culture. In summation, then, administrators need to model desired behavior and then reward it when it occurs. As a result, educational institutions will become what Peter Senge refers to as "learning organizations" (Senge, 1990).

DEVELOPING POSITIVE ATTITUDES

Another aspect of organizational behavior and culture is attitude formation. An attitude is a consistent predisposition to respond to various aspects of people, situations, or objects that are inferred from a person's behavior or expressed attitude, as well as from other cognitive, affective, or connotative responses. Attitudes are pervasive and predict behavior toward their objects. For instance, a leader might determine an individual's job satisfaction by inferring it from the employee's general demeanor on the job or by asking the person to describe this attitude.

Data can be formally and informally collected to support claims. Attitude surveys or other collections of attitude scales to assess individuals' attitudes toward their job, coworkers, supervisor, or the school or school system at large are often used in this way (Greenwald, 1989). Once again, being a change agent helps in developing an overall positive attitude within an educational institution.

IMPLICATIONS FOR PRACTICE: DEVELOPING ORGANIZATION CULTURE CASE STUDY

Lincoln Elementary School is located in a large, urban school district. Currently the school serves 575 students from K–5. The school's student body is predominantly comprised of black and brown students of African American, Caribbean Black, and Latinx communities.

Despite incremental increases in standardized test scores, Lincoln Elementary School remains on high alert that the school may be taken over by the state because of low literacy skills scores, as measured by the state's standardized testing program and by federal educational standards. The majority white teaching staff seem to be working diligently with a new district-imposed curriculum aimed at improving learning and, in turn, improving the test scores. In fact, the scores have been improving slightly throughout the current school year. Supplies, however, have been scarce, and the principal has been so anxious regarding the test scores that she has become more autocratic in her leadership style. The combination of limited resources and the principal's leadership approach has caused frustration among many of the faculty and staff.

The culture of Lincoln Elementary School is a rather complex combination of stress, denial, enthusiasm, and a strong work ethic. The overwhelming stressors are the implementation of a new curriculum and the specter of being immersed in the high-stakes testing environment created, in part, by federal guidelines and policy. As a result, during the current academic year, the teaching staff has an increased staff illness rate and the lowest teacher retention percentage among peer institutions in the city (especially for its faculty of color).

Another influence of the school's culture is the implementation of a new truancy policy. Now, parents who allow their child to stay home for more than three consecutive days are called and notified that someone will arrive at their doorstep the following day if the child does not report to school. This approach has decreased the instances of truancy but has alienated some caregivers, especially homesteads with two working adults and single-parent homes.

It is important that the entire school community cooperate and collaborate in addressing the educational deficiencies of the school and the school district. It is equally important that the school culture is trusting and respectful if improvement is to be had. A nimble culture that is tolerant of change will assist in reform efforts for significant improvement. The principal is aware that the school culture is not ideal for what lies ahead. What to do; what to do?

DIAGNOSTIC DEBRIEF

Here are some questions that can assess an institution's organizational culture:

- Does the organization exhibit a culture of mutual trust and respect?
- Do perceptual distortions proliferate?
- Does the workforce exhibit an internal locus of control?
- Is the institution a learning organization?
- Are the various learning styles being addressed in the management process?
- Is the leader adapting his or her leadership style to the learning style of the followers?
- What beliefs and values do the individuals in the organization have?
- How do these beliefs and values influence individual attitudes?
- What functional and dysfunctional behaviors result from the individuals' perceptions, attributions, learning, and attitudes?
- Are the leaders modeling desired behavior?

Chapter 3

Transformative Leadership Models

Leaders make themselves and others comfortable in a changing world. They eagerly explore new ideas, approaches, and cultures rather than shrink defensively from what lurks around life's next corner. Anchored by nonnegotiable principles and values, they cultivate the "indifference" that allows them to adapt confidently.

—Chris Lowney

Leadership is offered as a solution for most of the problems of organizations everywhere. Schools will work, it is often told, if principals provide strong instructional leadership. Organizations will be successful if they have visionary leaders. Around the world, administrators and managers say that their organizations would thrive if only senior management provided strategy, vision, and real leadership. Though the call for leadership is universal, there is much less clarity about what the term means (Kilpatrick and Locke, 1991).

Historically, researchers in this field have searched for the one best leadership style that would be most effective in all cases. Current thought, however, is that there is no one best style. Rather, a combination of styles depending on the situation in which the leader finds him- or herself has been found to be more appropriate. To understand the evolution of leadership theory thought, this chapter takes a historical approach and traces the progress of leadership theory beginning with the trait perspective of leadership and moving to the more current contingency theories of leadership.

Trait theory suggests that one can evaluate leadership and propose ways of leading effectively by considering whether an individual possesses certain personality traits, social traits, and physical characteristics. Popular in the 1940s and 1950s, trait theory attempted to predict which individuals successfully became leaders and then whether they were effective. Leaders differ from non-leaders in their drive, desire to lead, honesty and integrity, self-confidence, cognitive ability, and knowledge of their fields.

Limitations in the ability of traits to predict effective leadership caused researchers during the 1950s to view a person's *behavior* rather than that individual's personal traits as a way of increasing leadership effectiveness. This view also paved the way for later behavioral and situational theories.

The types of leadership behaviors investigated typically fell into two categories: production oriented and employee oriented. Production-oriented leadership, also called concern for production, initiating structure, or task-focused leadership, involves acting primarily to get the task done. An administrator who tells his or her science department chair to "do everything he or she needs to do to get the new ecology curriculum developed on time for the start of school, regardless of the personal consequences" demonstrates production-oriented leadership. The same is true for an administrator who uses an autocratic style or fails to involve workers in any aspect of decision-making. Employee-oriented leadership also called concern for people or collaborative leadership focuses on supporting the individual workers in their activities and involving the workers in decision-making. A principal who demonstrates great concern for his or her teachers' job satisfaction with their duties and is sensitive to both their personal and professional needs has an employee-oriented leadership style.

SITUATIONAL LEADERSHIP THEORY

Contingency or situational models differ from the earlier trait and behavioral models in asserting that no single way of leading works in all situations. Rather, appropriate behavior depends on the circumstances at a given time. Effective managers diagnose the situation, identify the leadership style that will be most effective, and then determine whether they can implement the required style.

Research suggests that the effect of leader behaviors on performance is altered by such intervening variables as the effort of subordinates, their ability to perform their jobs, the clarity of their job responsibilities, the organization of the work, the cooperation and cohesiveness of the group, the sufficiency of resources and support provided to the group, and the coordination of work group activities with those of other subunits. Thus, leaders must respond to these and broader cultural differences in choosing an appropriate style.

THE BOLMAN/DEAL MODEL

Bolman and Deal have developed a unique situational leadership theory that analyzes leadership behavior through four frames of reference: structural, human resource, political, and symbolic. Each of the frames offers a different perspective on what leadership is and how it operates in organizations. Each can result in either effective or ineffective conceptions of leadership (Bolman and Deal, 1991).

Structural leaders develop a new model of the relationship of structure, strategy, and environment for their organizations. They focus on implementation. The right answer helps only if it can be implemented. They are often referred to by their followers as direct, no nonsense, and hands on managers. Structural leaders sometimes fail because they miscalculate the difficulty of putting their design in place. They often underestimate the resistance that it will generate, and they take few steps to build a base of support for their innovations. In short, they are often undone by human resource, political, and symbolic considerations. Structural leaders do continually experiment, evaluate, and adapt, but because they fail to consider the entire environment in which they are situated, they sometimes are ineffective.

Human resource leaders believe in people and communicate that belief. They are passionate about "productivity through people." They demonstrate this faith in their words and actions and often build it into a philosophy or credo that is central to their vision of their organizations. Human resource leaders are visible and accessible. Peters and Waterman (Peters and Waterman, 1988) popularized the notion of "management wandering around," the idea that managers need to get out of their offices and interact with workers and customers. Many educational administrators have adopted this management principle.

Effective human resource leaders empower; that is, they increase participation, provide support, share information, and move decision-making as far down the organization as possible. Human resource leaders often like to refer to their employees as "partners" or "colleagues." They want to make it clear that employees have a stake in the organization's success and a right to be involved in making decisions. When they are ineffective, however, they are seen as naive or as weaklings and wimps.

Political leaders clarify what they want and what they can get. Political leaders are realists above all. They never let what they want cloud their judgment about what is possible. They assess the distribution of power and interests. The political leader needs to think carefully about the players, their interests, and their power; in other words, the leader must map the political terrain. Political leaders ask questions such as "Whose support do I need? How do I go about getting it? Who are my opponents? How much power do they have? What can I do to reduce the opposition? Is the battle winnable?" However, if ineffective, these leaders are perceived as being untrustworthy and manipulative.

The symbolic frame provides still a fourth turn of the kaleidoscope of leadership. In this frame, the organization is seen as a stage, a theater in which every actor plays certain roles and attempts to communicate the right impressions to the right audiences. The main premise of this frame is that whenever reason and analysis fail to contain the dark forces of ambiguity, human beings erect symbols, myths, rituals, and ceremonies to bring order, meaning, and predictability out of chaos and confusion.

Transforming leaders are visionary leaders, and visionary leadership is invariably symbolic. Examination of symbolic leaders reveals that they follow a consistent set of practices and rules. Transforming leaders use symbols to capture attention. For example, consider a principal of a charter school in Philadelphia who knew that she would face a substantial challenge. The school had all the usual problems of urban public schools: decaying physical plant, lack of student discipline, racial tension, troubles with the teaching staff, low morale, and limited resources. The only good news was that the situation was so bad that almost any change would be an improvement.

In the aforementioned situation, symbolic leaders will try to do something visible, even dramatic, to let people know that changes are on the way. Consider what if (during the summer before she assumed her duties), this principal wrote a letter to every teacher to set up an individual meeting. What if she traveled to meet teachers wherever they wanted, even if it meant driving two hours? And when meeting with staff she engaged in meaningful dialogue asking teachers how they felt about the school and what changes they wanted.

Still building on the same scenario, consider the principal also felt that something needed to be done about the dilapidated state of the school building. In response, she decides that the front door and some of the worst classrooms warrant repainting. She had no delusions about the challenges she would face getting through the bureaucracy of the Philadelphia public school system to provide painters, so she persuaded some of her family and local community members to help paint. When school opened, students and staff members immediately saw that things were going to be different, if only symbolically. Perhaps even more important, staff members received a subtle challenge to contribute themselves.

Moral framing can be used to view situational leadership theory and the Bolman/Deal model in tandem. Here, the moral frame completes situational leadership theory. Without it, leaders could just as easily use their leadership skills for promoting evil as for promoting good. Leaders operating out of the moral frame are concerned about their obligations to their followers. Moral frame leaders use some type of moral compass to direct their behavior. They practice what has been described as servant leadership and are concerned with those individuals and groups that are marginalized in their organizations and in society. In short, they are concerned about equality, fairness, and social justice. The moral frame is explored in more detail in chapter 11 (Palestini, 2012).

LEADERSHIP BEHAVIORS

Lest one be confused about what leadership behaviors fit into what frames, here are some examples:

Structural Frame Behaviors
- developing a vision
- setting goals
- developing a strategic plan
- implementing the plan
- proposing and implementing change in the form of improvements
- closely supervising followers
- developing rules and regulations
- developing job descriptions and responsibilities
- striving for the magis (continuous improvement, seeking, and reaching for more/greater)
- demonstrating competency (knowledgeable, organized, industrious, passionate, committed)
- hands on managing
- attending to detail
- lifelong learning
- meticulously preparing
- behaving authoritatively
- using analytical and logical thinking
- mastering the technical aspects of one's profession

Human Resource Frame Behaviors
- developing a system of rewards to motivate employees
- giving praise for accomplishments
- empowering others
- concern for the individual, the whole person (cura personalis)
- participative decision-making
- team building
- acknowledging special occasions (e.g., birthdays, anniversaries, get well sentiments)
- managing by walking around (being visible)

Symbolic Frame Behaviors

- concern for one's personal appearance
- modeling desired behavior
- motivational speeches and publications
- inspirational quotes, slogans, adages, and so on (on letterhead/posters)
- displaying symbols of achievement in the workplace
- telling stories, jokes, and so on
- being visible

Political Frame Behaviors

- negotiating a contract or covenant on compensation and working conditions
- lobbying for improvements
- fund-raising and institutional development activities
- making compromises (quid pro quo)
- building political and social capital
- engaging in a force-field analysis (neutralizing opposing forces) to effect change

Moral Frame Behaviors

- developing a personal moral compass to guide one's behavior
- striving for the magis (the greater good, striving for excellence)
- modeling personal integrity and moral character (being honest and forthright)
- being sensitive to the human needs of all (cura personalis), especially the marginalized in the workplace
- being concerned about equality, fairness, and social justice in the workplace and in society

THE HERSEY/BLANCHARD MODEL

In an attempt to integrate previous knowledge about leadership into a prescriptive model of leadership style, this model cites the "readiness of followers," defined as their ability and willingness to accomplish a specific task, as the major contingency that influences appropriate leadership style (Hersey and Blanchard, 1988). Follower readiness incorporates the follower's level of achievement motivation, ability, and willingness to assume responsibility for their own behavior in accomplishing specific tasks, and education and

Leader Behavior

Readiness Level III Participating Style	Readiness Level II Selling Style
Readiness Level IV Delegating Style	Readiness Level I Telling Style

Follower Readiness

Level IV	Level III	Level II	Level I
seasoned veteran and/or very secure	much experience and/or secure	some experience and/or confidence	inexperienced and/or insecure

Figure 3.1 Readiness of Followers Model.

experience relevant to the task. The model combines task and relationship behavior to yield four possible styles, as shown in figure 3.1.

Leaders should use a telling style, and provide specific instructions and closely supervise performance, when followers are unable and unwilling or insecure (R1). Leaders should use a selling style, and explain decisions and provide opportunity for clarification, when followers have moderate-to-low readiness (R2). Using a participating style, where the leader shares ideas and helps facilitate decision-making, should occur when followers have moderate-to-high readiness (R3). Finally, leaders should use a delegating style, and give responsibility for decisions and implementation to followers, when followers are able, willing, and confident (R4).

Although some researchers have questioned the conceptual clarity, validity, robustness, and utility of the model, as well as the instruments used to measure leadership style, others have supported the utility of the theory. For example, the Leadership Effectiveness and Description (LEAD) Scale and related instruments, developed to measure leadership style by Hersey and Blanchard, are widely used in industrial training programs. This model can easily be adapted to educational administration and be used analytically to understand leadership deficiencies and to prescribe the appropriate style for a variety of situations.

Transformational Leadership

Transformational leaders are situational, but are also able to use their personal charisma to inspire their followers. They talk to their followers about how essential their performance is, how confident they are in the followers, how exceptional the followers are, and how he or she expects the group's performance to exceed expectations. Warren Buffett, Jack Welsh, and Bill Gates in industry, Marie Montessori, the late Marcus Foster, and former Notre Dame president, Reverend Theodore Hesburgh are examples in education of this type of leader. Such leaders use dominance, self-confidence, a need for influence, and conviction of moral righteousness to increase their charisma and consequently their leadership effectiveness.

A transformational leader changes an organization by recognizing an opportunity and developing a vision, communicating that vision to organizational members, building trust in the vision, and achieving the vision by motivating organizational members. The leader helps subordinates recognize the need for revitalizing the organization by developing a felt need for change, overcoming resistance to change, and avoiding quick-fix solutions to problems.

Encouraging subordinates to act as devil's advocates with regard to the leader, building networks outside the organization, and visiting other organizations also help them recognize a need for revitalization. The transformational leader creates a new vision and mobilizes commitment to it by planning or educating others. They build trust through demonstrating personal expertise, self-confidence, and personnel integrity. Finally, the transformational leader must institutionalize the change by replacing old technical, political, cultural, and social networks with new ones.

A transformational leader motivates subordinates to achieve beyond their original expectations by increasing their awareness about the importance of designated outcomes and ways of attaining them, by getting workers to go beyond their self-interest to that of the team, the school, the school system, and the larger society, by changing or expanding the individual's needs. Subordinates report that they work harder for such leaders. In addition, such leaders are judged higher in leadership potential by their subordinates as compared to the more common transactional leader.

One should be cognizant, however, to the negative side of charismatic leadership which may exist if the leader overemphasizes devotion to him- or herself, makes personal needs paramount, or uses highly effective communication skills to mislead or manipulate others. Such leaders may be so driven to achieve a vision that they ignore the costly implications of their goals. The superintendent who over expands his or her jurisdiction in an effort to form an "empire," only to have the massive system turn into a bureaucratic nightmare, is an example of transformational leadership gone sour. Nevertheless, recent research has verified the overall effectiveness of transformational leadership style.

MISSION-CENTRIC LEADERSHIP

A community, collaborative approach to school mission development is key to its success and adoption by stakeholders. The intentionality of the mission is also very important for consideration as it sets the stage for the success that is expected to come as a result of acting upon it. When a leader espouses the words driving the work of the organization, they are harnessing a mission-centric leadership style. While this style is also known in different fields as mission-driven leadership, the tenets remain the same: utilizing the organization's collective purpose and vision to inform governance, leadership, strategy, culture, community impact, programing, and future direction.

It has been said that better outcomes are directly linked to fulfilling the promises of the mission statement. Leaders with this focus are not task oriented. This difference implores mission-centric leaders to be moral agents of change, rather than purveyors of simply task mastery. In a school setting, this leadership style might influence practices where the organization's mission and vision statements are visible throughout the facilities, meeting agenda begin with a centering exercise about mission-related mindedness, and/or utilizing the institutional mission statement as a way to determine the most appropriate resolution to a difficult decision. Importantly, mission-centric leadership is often linked to mission-driven learning initiatives, pedagogical practice, and people-centered leadership mindedness.

INSTRUCTIONAL LEADERSHIP MODEL

Instructional leadership as defined by the National Association of Elementary School Principals (2001) is a practice guiding the way learning communities are developed and led. Within this praxis, staff members regularly meet to discuss their work, collaborate in problem-solving, reflect on their profession, and hold themselves accountable for student learning.

Given this definition might seek one to ask what is a school leader's responsibly as an instructional leader? Murphy (1988) also outlines four major dimensions of instructional leadership and the responsibilities of leaders who serve under this model: they are (1) mission, vision, and goal development, (2) curriculum and instruction management, (3) academic learning climate monitoring and promotion, and (4) work environment stability and growth. While these dimensions can be executed linearly, they are often approached in tandem and/or a non-sequential order.

Instructional leaders often work with individual teachers to assist in pedagogical improvement, modeling instructional strategies, teacher observation, co-teaching, co-planning lessons and units, and giving critical feedback for success. Within this practice, coaching is known to be an important component to instructional leadership. The current widespread practice of professional learning communities (PLCs) in K–12 education is said to have derived from instructional leadership models.

AN EFFECTIVE LEADERSHIP FORMULA

For the concrete/sequential thinkers, it is oftentimes clearer and more understandable if a complex theory such as situational leadership theory can be placed in mathematical terms. The following is my attempt to do so:

$$\text{Effective Leadership Behavior} = (\text{is a function of}) \frac{St + Hr + Pl + Sy(\text{Moral})}{\text{Readiness}}$$

where St represents structural frame behavior, Hr characterizes human resource behavior, Pl is political frame behavior, Sy denotes symbolic frame behavior, Moral represents moral frame behavior, and Readiness signifies the maturity (the ability and willingness to perform the task) level of the follower(s).

Thus, one would articulate this formula in the following manner: Effective leadership behavior is the result of or the function of the appropriate application of one or some combination of structural, human resource, political, and symbolic frame behavior, depending on the readiness level of the followers, with the moral frame being a constant.

IMPLICATIONS FOR EDUCATION

The implications of leadership theory for educational administrators are rather clear. The successful administrator needs to have a sound grasp of leadership theory and the skills to implement it. The principles of situational and transformational leadership theory are guides to effective administrative behavior. The leadership behavior applied to an inexperienced faculty member may be significantly different than that applied to a more experienced and tested one. Task behavior or structural frame behavior may be appropriate in dealing with a new teacher, while relationship behavior or human resource frame behavior may be more appropriate when dealing with a seasoned teacher.

The four frames of leadership discussed by Bolman and Deal may be particularly helpful to school administrators. Consideration of the structural, human relations, political, and symbolic implications of leadership behavior can keep an administrator attuned to the various dimensions affecting appropriate leadership behavior. With the need to deal with collective bargaining entities, school boards, and a variety of other power issues, the political frame considerations may be particularly helpful in understanding the complexity of relationships that exist between administrators and these groups. Asking oneself the questions posed earlier under the political frame can be an effective guide to the appropriate leadership behavior in dealing with these groups. The Hersey/Blanchard model, on the other hand, may be particularly enlightening in recognizing the importance of employee readiness level and the need to adapt one's leadership style to the readiness level of the follower.

Recently, a plethora of research studies have been conducted on leadership and leadership styles. The overwhelming evidence indicates that there is no one singular leadership style that is most appropriate in all situations. Rather, an administrator's leadership style should be adapted to the situation so that at various times task behavior or relationship behavior might be appropriate. At other times and in other situations, various degrees of both task and relationship behavior may be most effective.

The emergence of transformational leadership has seen leadership theory come full circle. Transformational leadership theory combines aspects of the early trait theory perspective with the more current situational or contingency models. The personal charisma of the leader, along with his or her ability to formulate an educational vision and to communicate it to others determines the transformational leader's effectiveness.

Since the effective leader is expected to adapt his or her leadership style to an ever-changing environment, administration becomes an even more complex and challenging task. However, a thorough knowledge of leadership theory can make some sense of the apparent chaos that the administrator faces on almost a daily basis.

IMPLICATIONS FOR PRACTICE: TRANSFORMATIVE LEADERSHIP MODELS CASE STUDY

The Harrison County Intermediate Unit (HCIU) is an educational service agency serving the eighteen school districts of Harrison County, Delaware. It provides numerous programs for school district staff on many levels, from the board rooms and administrative offices to the classroom. In addition, the HCIU works with teachers and other staff to coordinate student activities, such as spelling bees and student leadership programs, on county and regional levels. HCIU's strength as an institution is the result of its being able to adapt to these changes—in funding, technology, educational research, and other areas—and, in many ways, anticipating changes and preparing school district leaders and staffs for the challenges ahead.

The HCIU's Board of Directors consists of eighteen members, one from each of its constituent school districts, and meets twice a month. There is also a Chiefs' Council made up of the eighteen district superintendents who "advise" the executive director on matters relative to programs and budgets impacting school districts.

Ronald A. Maker (RAM), executive director of the Intermediate Unit, has been with the HCIU since 1983, the year intermediate units (IUs) were created. Starting as an instructional materials service (IMS) program specialist, he advanced up the management ladder through supervisor and assistant executive director, and in 1997 he became executive director. Every five years since, his contract has been renewed by the board. He plans to retire at the end of this next cycle.

RAM currently has a harmonious relationship with the board and has had one since his appointment in 1997. However, his relationship with the superintendents is not always so harmonious. In fact, a faction of the superintendents' group actively campaigned against his reappointment. His predecessor had been a gentle manager, keeping peace at all costs among the eighteen superintendents.

Differently than his predecessor, RAM is viewed as a very aggressive, task-oriented leader, more akin to a businessman, as attested by the excellent financial status of HCIU in times when other IUs were floundering and their very existence was questioned. He has an entrepreneurial approach, and this vision has led the HCIU into diversified services, including digital literacy, tax billing, management information services, and computer game design, to name just a few. He views the HCIU as a business.

Once monthly, the cabinet (executive director, assistant executive director, management services director, and human resources director) meet in a research and development (R&D) session to explore new avenues of products and services. The assistant executive director has responsibility for the educational and social services programs.

In contrast to RAM, the assistant executive director is a relational leader, although when needed they can be a task-oriented leader. The assistant executive director is well respected by the board and the superintendents for their knowledge of curriculum, strategic planning, and current trends in education. RAM depends on them greatly to be on the "cutting edge" of educational developments.

The director of management services (business manager) and the human resources director serve as "gatekeepers," keeping the finances and legal, contractual houses in order, while also serving the districts by keeping them up to date on financial and legal issues, respectively. RAM gives his top management team much leeway in their areas of expertise. To employees lower down the organization chart, RAM is somewhat feared. He is a very direct, bottom-line manager and in the past, as assistant executive director under a kinder, gentler executive director, often had to be the hatchet man.

The present governor's agenda includes, along with vouchers, another hot topic—charter schools. Although the legislature has not even passed a bill (yet) authorizing charter schools, $1 million in seed money (grants of $100,000) is available from the Delaware Department of Education to school districts, community agencies, parents, institutions of higher learning, and others to pilot charter schools.

RAM, unlike his superintendent counterparts, did not merely dismiss vouchers or charter schools as the agenda of an anti-public education governor but sees these as a business opportunity for the HCIU. A voucher system would need a middleman—a broker—to implement such a system, a perfect fit for IUs, who already serve as an "intermediary" between the Delaware Department of Education and 113 public school districts and numerous private schools.

At the last superintendents' meeting, RAM proposed that the districts and HCIU form a consortium, apply for the planning grants, pool their seed money, and plot an alternative education charter school for elementary students. Although alternative education programs for secondary students are common, such programs for elementary students are not.

Reaching troubled youth in the third, fourth, fifth, and sixth grades with alternative education programs may "catch" them before more serious trouble occurs and more drastic actions are necessary. Although many of the superintendents agree with the concept, they are absolutely against HCIU spearheading such a charter school program. For the IU to do so would be cooperating with a governor whom the superintendents believe wishes to destroy public education. At the last Chief's Council meeting, the superintendents told RAM that if he pursued a grant for HCIU to start a charter school, he would be setting up the IU in an adversarial role with the school districts, and they would not send any students to the pilot charter school.

RAM was angry with the superintendents. He believed that some of the governor's criticism of public educators is deserved. They "don't see the handwriting on the wall," RAM told the HCIU board (made up of one member from each district) about how the superintendents feel. Several board members are angry that the superintendents squelched the idea without consulting their boards. Some board members feel that each district board, not the superintendents, should evaluate what ventures the district goes into with HCIU.

DIAGNOSTIC DEBRIEF

Here are some questions that may be helpful in assessing the effectiveness of the leadership in an institution:

- What necessary behaviors required for effective leadership must administrators display?
- How do school leaders encourage the appropriate amount of participation in decision-making?
- How must leadership adapt their leadership behavior to the readiness levels of the followers?
- What attributes must be embraced for effective transformation, a process seeking continuous improvement?
- What benefits might come from leaders operating in all five frames of organization leadership?

Chapter 4

Motivation for Change

Exceptional people convert life's setbacks into future successes. . . .
With the right mindset and the right teaching, people are capable of a
lot more than we think.

—Carol Dweck

Fueling much discourse in the last decade is the debate regarding student achievement. How should such be measured? Some scholars support rankings, ratings, and percentages of student proficiency based on calculations across standardized measures, while those in opposition argue for a holistic evaluation of student growth. Exploring a hope-filled promise provided by the latter, the work of Dweck's model of growth mindset, serves as a backdrop for investigating the differences between fixed and growth mindsets.

GROWTH MINDSET

People feel comfortable with dichotomous choices; that is, they often prefer situations where dualistic options help narrow selects to just two considerations. So, while there may be arguably many alternative choices from which to choose, there is comfort in a simplistic model of dualistic comparison. Carol Dweck employs this premise in her model for mindset.

Simplistically, Dweck's (2008) mindset model explains that there are two differences between the way a person approaches difficult challenges. Those who prescribe to fixed-mindedness believe talents are innate gifts. Differently, growth mindset refers to talent development through perseverance, dedication, strategic planning, and collaboration from and with others.

An example of leading with growth mindset is articulating the belief of a future skill acquisition in saying, "not yet" after failing to complete a seemingly insurmountable task. One might hear this in a second-grade math class when a student replies, "I'm no good at subtraction," and the teacher responds, "not yet" or a star athlete fails to successfully complete a high bar jump and is reminded by their coach, "not yet." This ostensibly simple phrase reestablishes a *can-do* attitude and focus.

Although differences between fixed and growth mindsets may appear nuanced, they matter. Of considerable interest is the role of *effort*. The belief that effort can lead to mastery of a new skill provides opportunity to explore failure as an essential part of the learning process. Explained as temporary setbacks, failure is often expected as an outcome of trying something new, but more importantly, is deemed necessary for growth. Combined with attributes for embracing challenges, accepting critical feedback from others, and the inclination to be motivated by and learn from the success of others, leaders with a growth mindset are poised for success.

PRAISE AND REPRIMAND

Blanchard and Johnson suggest that managers utilize praising and reprimanding as motivational devises in an organization. This flows from their first "secret" of effective management, goal-setting. Goal-setting theory suggests that setting difficult, but attainable goals that are mutually agreed upon can be a powerful motivator (Blanchard and Johnson, 1982).

Setting goals like higher reading scores on standardized tests or lower teacher absenteeism or a higher graduation rate help focus behavior and motivate individuals to achieve the desired end. However, in order for goal-setting to be an effective motivator, the individual involved needs feedback on whether movement toward attaining the goal is adequately progressing. This is where praise and reprimands come into play. It is important that the administrator keep their staff abreast of the adequacy of employee performance. When they are very specific and clear, both praise and reprimands can be effective sources of motivation. As Blanchard and Johnson point out, however, one should "never attack a person's worth or value as a person" (Blanchard and Johnson, 1982, p. 17).

Reprimand the "behavior" only, not the "person." Thus, the feedback and the individual's reaction to it are about the specific behavior and not their feelings about themselves as human beings. It is always a good idea to follow or precede a reprimand with a praising. Make certain that the staff member knows that their behavior is not okay, but that they are okay. In religious terms, the advice is to "hate the sin and love the sinner." According to Blanchard and Johnson, the one-minute manager should not be Nice 'n' Tough, but rather, Tough 'n' Nice (Blanchard and Johnson, 1982, p. 32).

Reinforcement theory applies behaviorist learning theories to motivation and has implications for the effectiveness of praise and reprimands (Thorndike, 1938). This theory emphasizes the importance of feedback and rewards in motivating desired behavior through diverse reinforcement techniques, including positive reinforcement, like praise, and negative reinforcement, like reprimands.

Positive reinforcement involves actively encouraging a desired behavior by repeated praise of desired behaviors or outcomes with rewards or feedback. This feedback "shapes" behavior by encouraging the reinforced or rewarded behavior to recur. If the behavior is not precisely what is desired by the administrator, repeated reinforcements resulting in successive approximations to the desired behavior can move the actual behavior closer to the desired behavior. For example, if a principal desires more interactive classroom instruction of a teacher, the principal might compliment the teacher when a cooperative learning activity is part of the lesson plan, and when other interactive techniques are used, additional praise may be given. Praise and other incentives are used until the best performance occurs.

Punishment, on the other hand, actively eliminates undesirable behaviors by applying an undesirable reinforcer (reprimand) to an undesirable behavior. Although it can be effective in eliminating undesirable behavior, punishment can produce anger and bitterness and be counterproductive in the long run.

Based on the negative after effects of punishment, the administrator must be careful to reprimand infrequently, and when doing so, to reprimand the undesirable behavior and not the individual. It is also the reason why, when possible, a reprimand of the behavior should be followed by or preceded a praising of the individual. "Your lesson plan for today was somewhat poorly conceived, but I know that you have the ability to do better" is an example of reprimanding the behavior and praising the individual. Goal-setting theory and praising and reprimanding are just two of the ways to motivate faculty and staff. There are a number of other ways of doing so.

NEEDS THEORIES

Suppose the superintendent of a school district makes $200,000 a year and a typical teacher earns $55,000. And suppose this district decided to base part of its annual salary increases on whether the school met its student achievement goals (measured by standardized test scores). Why would such a district think this policy might motivate its employees? Early motivation theorists would explain such a situation by saying that the district expects the new policy to meet the employees' *needs*—their basic requirements for living and working productively.

How does one identify employees' needs? To do a good job of identifying them, the leader probably would need to spend a great deal of time talking with the employees and observing their behavior both in and out of the work environment. Many times, determining employees' needs outside of the work environment is conjecture. In the example given earlier, one might conjecture that such a policy might meet the employees' achievement motive.

In this section, two seminal (and widely popular) needs theories are presented: Maslow's hierarchy-of-needs theory and William Glasser's control theory. Each of these theories describes a specific set of needs the researchers believe individuals have, and each differs somewhat in the number and kinds of needs identified.

Maslow's Hierarchy of Needs Theory

In 1935, Abraham Maslow developed the first needs theory, and it is still one of the most popular and well-known motivation theories. Maslow stated that individuals have five needs, arranged in a hierarchy from the most basic to the highest level, as shown in figure 4.1: physiological, safety and security, belongingness and love, esteem, and self-actualization (Maslow, 1987).

Physiological needs are the most basic needs an individual has. These include, at a minimum, a person's requirement for food, water, shelter, and the ability to care for his or her family. Providing employees with a living wage and medical and dental coverage would help satisfy this need. Safety needs include a person's desire for security or protection. This translates most directly into concerns for short-term and long-term job security, as well as physical safety at work. Sense of belonging and the need for love focus on the social aspects of work and non-working situations.

Virtually all individuals desire affectionate relationships or regular interaction with others, which can become a key facet of job design. Esteem needs relate to a person's desire to master his or her work, demonstrate competence, build a reputation as an outstanding performer, hold a position of prestige, receive public recognition, and feel self-confident. Self-actualization needs reflect an individual's desire to grow and develop to his or her fullest potential. An individual often wants the opportunity to be creative on the job or desires autonomy, responsibility, and challenge.

According to needs theory, organizations must meet unsatisfied needs in order to motivate their employees. In Maslow's scheme, the lowest unsatisfied need, starting with the basic physiological needs and continuing through safety, belonging and love, esteem, and self-actualization needs, becomes the prepotent or most powerful and significant need.

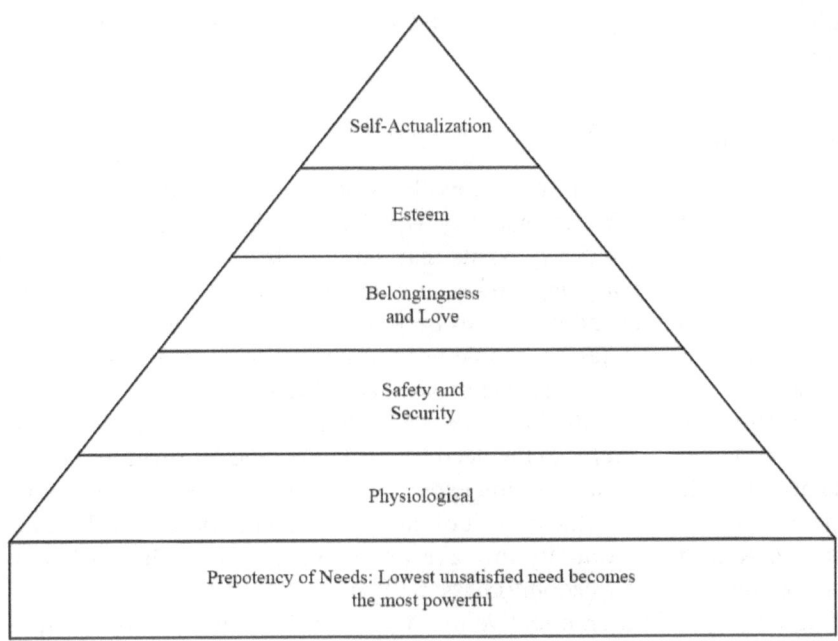

Figure 4.1 Maslow's Hierarchy of Needs.

Although the order may vary in certain special circumstances, generally the prepotent need motivates an individual to act to fulfill it; satisfied needs do not motivate. If, for example, a person lacks sufficient food and clothing, he or she will act to satisfy those basic physiological needs; hence, this person would most likely work to receive pay or other benefits to satisfy those needs. On the other hand, a person whose physiological, safety, and belongingness needs are satisfied will be motivated to satisfy needs at the next level, the esteem needs. For this person, pay will not motivate performance unless it increases esteem, by a promotion or other changes in a job's title or status.

Consider again the example of the college that attached some of the salary increases to whether the college reached its recruitment goals. Using Maslow's theory to diagnose the likely effectiveness of the new policy, three questions can be asked: (1) Which needs have already been satisfied? (2) Which unsatisfied need is lowest in the hierarchy? (3) Can those needs be satisfied with the new policy? If, for example, the physiological and safety needs have been satisfied, then the social needs become prepotent; if the new policy can satisfy those needs, which is unlikely, then, according to Maslow's theory, it would be motivating. In this example, then, it is likely that the new policy would satisfy the teachers and administrators achievement or self-esteem needs.

Control Theory

William Glasser suggests that individuals strive to gain control over their emotions and behavior so that they will have healthier and more productive lives. His control theory posits that individuals are born with five basic human needs: survival, love, power, fun, and freedom. These needs must be satisfied in order for individuals to be productive in their work and private lives. According to Glasser, people need to control their own behavior so as to make the most need-satisfying choices possible.

The survival need is the innate desire of individuals to be safe and secure. Love and belonging refer to the need for affiliation and affirmation. Power is the need to obtain knowledge and expertise. To Glasser, knowledge is power. The inalienable right to the pursuit of happiness is an effort to fulfill the need for fun. And the opportunity to make free choices is what Glasser believes satisfies the need for freedom (Glasser, 1984).

According to Glasser, effective managers will see that these five needs are satisfied if his or her employees are expected to be productive. Coercion and competition are counterproductive. Quality performance, therefore, cannot be achieved in an adversarial setting. Workers will perform if coerced, but they will not perform in a quality manner. Competition enables one person to succeed while others fail. Cooperation, on the other hand, allows many winners.

Although Glasser's control theory has not been verified by empirical research, it has been demonstrated to be successful in a number of school system settings including the Johnson City, New York, school district, where standardized achievement test scores increased dramatically while Glasser's techniques were being used. The faculty was also judged to be more productive when programs were implemented that satisfied the five basic needs.

UTILIZATION OF NEEDS THEORIES

Despite some caveats, needs theory can be utilized effectively in educational settings. When an administrator is developing or refining the overall school program and organizational goals, they should analyze each component with the various needs in mind to be certain that some aspect of the activity or policy addresses one or more of the common needs. For example, if a teacher is preparing a lesson, they should go through Glasser's or another theorist's needs, to see if the lesson addresses the learner's needs for survival, love, power, fun, and freedom. In the same way, if an administrator is implementing a total quality management initiative or some other organizational development program at their institution, the administrator should incorporate facets that would satisfy each of the faculty and staff's needs in some significant way.

GOAL-SETTING THEORY

Although extensive research has been conducted on the goal-setting process and its relationship to performance, this section highlights only a sample of the findings. Goals, which any member of an organization can set, describe a desired future state, such as lower absenteeism, higher standardized test scores, higher teacher and staff satisfaction, or specified performance levels. Once established, they can focus behavior and motivate individuals to achieve the desired end state (Vance and Colella, 1990).

Goals can vary in at least three ways: specificity, difficulty, and acceptance. The specificity or clarity of goals refers to the extent to which their accomplishment is observable and measurable. "Reducing absenteeism by 20 percent" is a highly specific goal for a school; "all children achieving" is a much less specific goal. Goal difficulty, or the level of performance desired, can also vary significantly. A superintendent of schools might set a goal to recruit 10 percent more of the school aged children in his or her school district or to increase standardized test scores by 10 percent; the first goal might be relatively easy, the second extremely difficult.

Although goal-setting research originally called for setting moderately difficult goals, now empirical studies indicate that a linear relationship exists between goal difficulty and performance. Empirical studies that combined the two characteristics of goal specificity and difficulty showed that better performance accompanied specific difficult goals than vague, non-quantitative ones. Individuals' acceptance of stated goals, or their commitment to accomplishing the goals, may vary. In general, a subordinate is less likely to accept a goal as his or her own and try to accomplish it if a manager assigns the goal rather than jointly sets it with the subordinate (Latham and Yukl, 1975).

REDESIGN OF WORK

Work redesign modifies specific jobs to increase both the quality of the employees' work experience and the performance. Jobs, as a central concern in work design, are defined simply as a set of tasks grouped together under one job title; for example, teacher, principal, dean, and custodian are designed to be performed by a single individual. Moreover, jobs are bureaucratic, they are part of the organization, they exist independently of job incumbents, and they are relatively static.

Jobs do change, but not on a day-to-day basis. As a strategy for motivation and change, then, work-redesign programs alter the content and process of jobs to match the work motivation of individuals. That is, work-redesign efforts modify the school organization to enhance educator and student motivation. The approach to work redesign that will be considered here is career ladders.

CAREER LADDERS

As a redesign of educational work, career-ladder programs are seen by many policymakers as moving teaching careers closer to the professional end of the occupational continuum. Career ladders became one of the most touted and widely mandated reforms of teaching and schools during the 1980s and remnants of it continue to exist today. Such programs seek to ensure leadership sustainability and succession planning.

Three reasons are generally offered as rationale for creating career-ladder programs. The first is based on the research finding that many of the best teachers leave their instructional careers after a brief foray in the classroom. Historically, about 50 percent of a teacher cohort will leave teaching during the first six years. This percentage is even higher among people of color within the profession. Moreover, a disproportionate percentage of those leaving teaching are considered the most talented among their peers.

The second reason given for redesign is based on the observation that teaching in the elementary and secondary schools has a flat career path. Teachers have limited opportunities for advancement in their instructional work. New and experienced teachers have the same role expectations. Teachers with motivations to advance or gain new responsibilities generally have two choices; they can remain frustrated in their self-contained classrooms or they can leave.

A third reason supporting the need of career ladders is that, although teaching is demanding work requiring creativity and versatility, it is repetitive. Despite the variety of classroom challenges and achievements, one year can look very much like the next and there is little prospect to change the year-to-year pattern. Hence, career-ladder programs were seen as ways to attract and retain highly talented individuals to education (Hart, 1987).

A career-ladder program redesigns jobs to provide individuals with prospects for promotion, formalizes status ranks for teachers, matches teacher abilities with job tasks, and shares the responsibilities for school and faculty improvements with the professional staff. In essence, the goal of career-ladder programs is to enrich work and enlarge teacher responsibilities. Career ladders, as job-enrichment models, generally include promotions to higher ranks with the assumption of additional duties at each higher step. For example, mentoring and supervising new teachers, developing curriculum materials, and evaluating programs are typical. A more creative and attractive version of a career ladder is to provide teachers with an avenue to obtaining their doctorates so they can move to higher education later in their careers.

IMPLICATIONS FOR PRACTICE: MOTIVATION FOR CHANGE CASE STUDY

Sam Henson is relatively new to Yurlin Middle School (YMS). He remains early in his teaching career and he is still untenured. Like many recent college graduates in the teaching profession, he came full of energy and with high expectations to YMS. In his second year of teaching, it is a typical 8 a.m. start as the young Sam Henson closes the door to his car and begins his walk to the graffiti-covered YMS. There is a grim look on his face, and you can see distinctly the disgust and tiredness in Sam's eyes. As he walks up the concrete stairs leading to the entrance of YMS, he kicks away some of the usual garbage strewn in his path.

Sam opens the door and walks inside, where he is greeted by a nonteaching assistant (NTA). "Good Morning, Mr. Henson." Sam puts on his friendliest face and acknowledges the NTA with a "Hello." As he stands there, a few school children come running by. Sam yells, "Slow down!" The children ignore him and continue running. He walks into the mail room and then the main office. Sam signs in at the desk and says "Hello" to a few colleagues, who lazily walk in. He then walks out of the office and begins the dreaded daily journey to his classroom.

On his way to the classroom, Sam stops to talk with a fellow colleague, Mrs. Bowens. Mrs. Bowens privately converses with Sam and informs him that she is putting in for a transfer from Yurlin and cannot wait until the end of the year. Sam shakes his head and responds,

> I don't blame you. I have to wait until the end of the year before I can get out of this zoo. I will not make it eight years here, like yourself. I would not wait another minute if I were you. Especially after the way Mr. Wayward, the school principal, rudely shrugged off your question yesterday at the staff meeting. That just shows he does not care about any of us. I don't know who he thinks he is. We are in the classroom, doing whatever it takes to try and teach these kids something, and he is playing around in his office on the computer. We are trying our best with some of the toughest kids to teach in America and he rudely shrugs

you off like that. . . . This is not to mention the fact that we have few supplies, no books, not enough desks, burnt-out lights hanging in the room, busted windows, and everything else that is wrong with this ridiculous building. I have no energy as it is, trying to deal with these kids; the last thing I need to see is the school principal shrugging off my colleagues. Yeah, he cares.

Mrs. Bowens listens and shakes her head up and down. "You're right, Sam. You're right. I used to have the will to put up with everything for the children, but not anymore. I just cannot fight the administration and the kids at the same time. Look around this place; everyone is so depressed it is ridiculous." Sam responds, "I know, it is very sad."

Sam continues down the hallway to his room and opens his classroom door, turns on the few lights that work, and begins to prepare for another drawn out day at Yurlin Middle School, all the while replaying the conversation he just had with Mrs. Bowen. Admittedly, he's indifferent about the news of her future departure. Although he's excited she's finally getting out, this only seems to exacerbate the realization that his freedom seems so far away.

DIAGNOSTIC DEBRIEF

Here are some questions that might be used to assess an institution's motivational processes:

- Do the rewards provided satisfy the variety of individual needs?
- Is a full range of motivational tools being used?
- Are rewards both internal and external?
- Are they applied equitably and consistently?
- Is reinforcement theory (praising and reprimanding) being employed effectively?
- Do individuals set goals as a source of motivation (goal-setting theory)?
- Are the rewards and incentives effective in motivating desired behaviors?

Chapter 5

Relevance of Communication

It appears then that genuine friendship cannot exist where one of the parties is unwilling to hear the truth and the other is equally indisposed to speak it.

—Cicero

One of the perennial complaints of school personnel is a lack of communication between themselves and another segment of the school community. Oftentimes, the greatest perceived "communications gap" is between the faculty and the administration. If an administrator is to be effective, then, he or she must master the skill of effective communication.

COMMUNICATION MODELS AND MODES

There are many models used to explain communication processes, such as Aristotle's Model, Lasswell's Model, Shannon-Weaver Model, Berlo's S-M-C-R Model, Osgood-Schramm Model, the Westley and Maclean Model, Burnlund's Transactional Model, Dance's Helical Model, and so on (just to reference a few). Still, these models can be categorized into three types: linear, interactive, and transactional. Linear models seek to illustrate a one-directional communication process, whereas interactive types explore two-way interpersonal communication. The last type, transactional, is used to describe two-way immediate feedback communication processes.

Despite slight variations among each model type, certain components remain consistent. Simplistically, communication requires a sender, a receiver, and a message. Additional elements in communication processes may include the role of encoding/decoding, feedback, and environmental, cultural, and personal factors. Some components of these models are further described in this chapter.

Not only are there several communication model types to consider, but similarly, varying modes of communication remain available. A mode describes a means of communicating. When researching modal types, it is clear there is much variation in how scholars categorize and cluster types. For example, according to the New London Group, there are five multimodal types of communication: linguistic (written and spoken words), visual (images either moving or still), aural (sound), gestural (movement, expression, body language), and spatial (position, physical arrangement, proximity).

Another consideration organizes modes based on sharing information between individuals. Within this type, disseminating data takes place in one of three ways: interpretative (one-way), interpersonal (two-way), and presentational (one-way by addressing a group) communication. Other modal arrangements also exist.

In addition to contrasting models and modes of communication, the delivery method or device employed when communicating can vary. There are both verbal and nonverbal methods for consideration. Stories, literature, articles, speeches, songs, radio news, videos, and movies are most prevalent within an interpretative communication mode. Differently, in an interpersonal mode, social media, text messages, and telephones are often utilized. A presentational mode favors articles, flyers, short stories, reports, presentations, skits, debates, speeches, and so on to communicate.

Based on variabilities among different models, modes, and ways of communicating, it remains easy to understand why miscommunication is commonplace. Ensuring communication is concise and clearly understood by an intended receiver means successfully navigating a very complex labyrinth of choices.

COMMUNICATION EFFECTIVENESS

What can individuals do to improve their communication in both formal and informal settings? This section examines three ways of increasing communication effectiveness: creating a supportive communication climate, using an assertive communication style, and using active listening techniques.

In communicating with their faculties and staffs, administrators know they must create a trusting and supportive environment. Creating such a climate has the objective of shifting from attribution or blaming to problem-solving and staff development. Administrators must thus avoid making employees feel defensive, that is, feel threatened by the communication. They can create such an atmosphere in at least six tried and true ways (Zuker, 1938, p. 79):

1. They use descriptive rather than evaluative speech and do not imply that the receiver needs to change. An administrator may describe teacher traits in terms of strengths and areas in need of further development, rather than describing them as weaknesses.
2. They take a clinical approach, which implies a desire to collaborate in exploring a mutual problem, rather than trying to control or change the listener. An administrator can ask the teacher what he or she hopes to achieve in the lesson, or for the academic year, rather than setting out a list of preordained goals for the teacher.
3. They are spontaneous and honest, and reveal their goals, rather than appearing to use "strategy" that involves ambiguous and multiple motivations. A superintendent might share with the school community the need for restructuring and possible areas of downsizing rather than doing so surreptitiously, for example.
4. They convey empathy for the feelings of their listener, rather than appearing unconcerned or neutral about the listener's welfare. They give reassurance that they are identifying with the listener's problems, rather than denying the legitimacy of the problems. For example, when reviewing a union grievance with a teacher, the principal may indicate sensitivity to the teacher's position even though the decision may ultimately go against the teacher.
5. They indicate that they feel equal rather than superior to the listener. Thus, they suggest that they will enter a shared relationship, not simply dominate the interaction. A college dean may come out from behind his or her desk and sit next to a colleague to indicate a relationship of equality.
6. Finally, they communicate that they will be flexible regarding their own behavior and ideas, rather than be dogmatic about them. They do not give the impression that they know all the answers and do not need help from anyone. An administrator can concede that he or she does not know if his or her suggestion will work, but ask that the employee in question to "try it."

Another tested way of improving interpersonal communication is by encouraging individuals to communicate using as complete knowledge of themselves and others as possible. The Johari window provides an analytical tool that individuals can use to identify information that is available for use in communication. Table 5.1 illustrates this model of interpersonal knowledge (Gordon, 1993). Note that information about an individual is represented

Table 5.1 Johari Window.

	Known by Self	Unknown by Self
Known by Others	Open Self	Blind Self
Unknown by Others	Concealed Self	Unknown Self

along two dimensions: (1) information known and unknown by the self and (2) information known and unknown by others.

Together these dimensions form a four-category representation of the individual. The open self is information known by the self and known by others. The blind self is information unknown by the self and known by others, such as others' perceptions of your behavior or attitudes. The concealed self is information known by self and unknown by others; secrets kept from others fall into this category.

Finally, the unconscious self is information that is unknown to the self and unknown to others. To ensure quality communication, in most cases an individual should communicate from their "open self" to another's open self and limit the amount of information concealed or in the blind spot. Guarded communication may be appropriate, however, if one party has violated trust in the past, if the parties have an adversarial relationship, or if the relationship is transitory.

Assertive Communication Style

An assertive style, which is honest, direct, and firm, also improves communication. With this style a person expresses personal needs, opinions, and feelings in honest and direct ways and stands up for his or her rights without violating the other person's rights. Assertive behavior is reflected in the content and the nonverbal style of the message. The assertive leader, for example, is clear and direct when explaining work to subordinates, doesn't hover, and criticizes fairly, objectively, and constructively.

Consider the situation of a superintendent whose assistant has missed two important deadlines in the past month. How would she respond assertively? She might say to her assistant: "I know you missed the last two deadlines. Is there an explanation I should know? It is important that you meet the next deadlines." Your assertive response can include the expression of anger, frustration, or disappointment, but is couched in terms that would allow for feedback to obtain the employee's explanation for the behavior.

The assertive approach to nonassertive and aggressive styles can be further contrasted. Nonassertive communication describes behavior where the sender does not stand up for their leadership responsibilities and indicates that their feelings are unimportant; the person may be hesitant, apologetic, or fearful. In the situation of a missed deadline, nonassertive behavior might involve saying nothing to your assistant, hoping the situation would not recur. Individuals act non-assertively because they may mistake assertion for aggression, mistake non-assertion for politeness or being helpful, refuse to accept their leadership responsibilities, experience anxiety about negative consequences of assertiveness, or lack assertiveness skills (Palestini, 2012).

In aggressive communication one expresses his or her view and rights without respecting the rights of the other person. Aggressive behavior attempts to dominate and control others by sounding accusing or superior. In the situation of the missed deadlines, an aggressive response might be "You always miss deadlines. You're taking advantage of me and the situation. If you miss another deadline, disciplinary action will be taken." While such a response may result in the desired behavior in the short run, its long-term consequences likely will be dysfunctional, resulting in distrust between the individuals involved. Ultimately, such behavior will negatively affect productivity, and will especially affect the submission of creative and innovative solutions offered to management by the employee.

Active Listening Techniques

Active listening, which requires understanding both the content and the intent of a message, can be facilitated by paraphrasing, perception checking, and behavior description. The receiver can paraphrase the message conveyed by the sender by stating in his or her own way what the other person's remarks convey. For example, if the sender states "I don't like the work I am doing," the receiver might paraphrase it as, "Are you saying that you are dissatisfied with the profession of education?" "Or are you dissatisfied with the grade that you teach?" "Or do you wish to be reassigned to another school?" Note that these ways of paraphrasing the original message suggest very different understandings of the original statement. The sender, upon receiving this feedback from the receiver, can then clarify his or her meaning.

Alternatively, the receiver may perception check, that is, describe what he or she perceives as the sender's inner state at the time of communication to check his or her understanding of the message. For example, if the sender states, "I don't like the work I am doing," the receiver might check his or her perception of the statement by asking, "Are you dissatisfied with the tasks you have been given?" "Are you dissatisfied by the way you are being treated?" or, "Are you dissatisfied with me as a supervisor?" Note that answers to these two questions will identify different feelings.

A third way of checking communication is through behavior description. Here the individual reports specific, observable actions of others without making accusations or generalizations about their motives, personality, or characteristics. Similarly, description of feelings, where the individual specifies or identifies feelings by name, analogy, or some other verbal representation, can increase active listening. For example, in the instance cited earlier, one might ask of the speaker, "You look angry," "You look resentful," or "You seem bitter."

THE VALUE OF FEEDBACK

Along with a culture of trust and respect, feedback is perhaps the most important aspect of an effective communications process. Feedback refers to an acknowledgment by the receiver that the message has been received; it provides the sender with information about the receiver's understanding of the message being sent.

Often one-way communication occurs between administrators and their colleagues. Because of inherent power differences in their positions, administrators may give large quantities of information and directions to their faculty and staff without providing the opportunity for them to show their understanding or receipt of the information. These managers often experience conflict between their role as authorities and a desire to be liked and trusted by their colleagues.

Other administrators have relied almost exclusively on the use of written memoranda posted on the faculty/staff bulletin board as a way of communicating. In addition to the inherent lack of feedback involved in this format, the use of a single channel of communication also limits the effectiveness of communication. The proliferation of the use of email has alleviated this problem somewhat by providing a relatively facile feedback mechanism. Encouraging feedback from others, however, helps show them that leadership is concerned about them as individuals, in ways that go beyond merely ensuring that they produce.

EXTERNAL COMMUNICATION

As was discussed in chapter 1, the open system model of organizational structure highlights the vulnerability and interdependence of organizations and their environments. External environments are important because they affect the internal structures and processes of organizations; hence, one is forced to look both inside and outside the organization to explain behavior within school organizations.

However, the growing necessity to interact with the outside environment places added responsibilities and demands on the school district's communications processes. The need to communicate with parents, government officials, advocacy groups, and the mass media cannot be denied. This necessity, however, is a relatively recent phenomenon and presents difficulties to administrators whose training does not normally include communicating with the public through the mass media.

Although the principles of effective communication still prevail when dealing with the outside community, some nuances need to be stressed. Perhaps the most important aspect of communication that needs to be considered when dealing with the public is the uniformity of the message. The message must be clear and consistent and be emanating from a singular source. In these cases, the "chain of command" and "channels of communication" need to be well defined and structured along the lines of the classical model.

Given considerations in communication, it is imperative that the school "speak with one voice." Someone in the school district should be designated as the clearing house for all external communication. This individual, or office, should review all external communication for clarity and accuracy and school personnel should be keenly aware of the school's policy with regard to external communication. Thus, although a more loosely structured communication system is very appropriate for internal communications, a more tightly structured one is necessary for effective external communications.

MATRIX DESIGN

To overcome some of the problems of the classical chain of command structure of most organizations including schools, matrix or mixed designs have evolved to improve mechanisms of lateral communication and information flow across the organization (Lewis, 2005).

The matrix organization, originally developed in the aerospace industry, is characterized by a dual authority system. There are usually functional and program or product line managers, both reporting to a common superior and both exercising authority over workers within the matrix. Typically, a matrix organization is particularly useful in highly specialized technological areas that focus on innovation. Thus, schools, school systems, and institutions of higher education make ideal settings for matrix designs. Especially in interdisciplinary academic programs, the matrix structure facilitates the coordination of the team and allows team members to contribute their special expertise.

The matrix design has some disadvantages that stem from the dual authority lines. Individual workers may find having two supervisors to be untenable since it can create conflicting expectations and ambiguity. The matrix design may also be expensive in that both functional and program managers may spend a considerable amount of time at meetings attempting to keep everyone informed of program activities.

The use of matrix design in education is not very common, but it is a viable way of organizing when communication needs to occur outside the "proper channels." The popularity of interdisciplinary and multicultural courses and programs in education has caused an increased interest in matrix design. Many high schools and colleges are informally organized in a matrix design. It would most likely serve these institutions well to consider it as a formal organizational structure, especially in cases when communication problems are evident.

CONCLUSION

A foreign-born plumber in New York once wrote to the Bureau of Standards that he found hydrochloric acid fine for cleaning drains, and he asked if they agreed. Washington replied: "The efficacy of hydrochloric acid is indisputable, but the chlorine residue is incompatible with metallic permanence." The plumber wrote back that he was mighty glad the Bureau agreed with him. Considerably alarmed, the Bureau replied a second time: "We cannot assume responsibility for the production of toxic and noxious residues with hydrochloric acid, and suggest that you use an alternative procedure." The plumber was happy to learn that the Bureau still agreed with him. Whereupon Washington wrote: "Don't use hydrochloric acid; it eats hell out of pipes."

Communication with ease and clarity is no simple task and such can be even more cumbersome as greater reliance on digital communication in today's learning environment continues to increase. There are, however, various orientations toward how communication can be most effectively carried out. Classical theory, social system theory, and open system theory (chapter 1) all incorporate a perspective toward the communication process; or, who should say what through which channel to whom and toward what effect. Classical theory stresses that the communication process exists to facilitate the manager's command and control over the employees in a formal, hierarchical, and downwardly directed manner. The purpose is to increase efficiency and productivity.

The social system orientation suggests that to be effective, communication has to be two-way and that the meaning of the message is as much to be found in the psychological makeup of the receiver as it is the sender. The open system orientation emphasizes the communication process working toward drawing the various subsystems of an organization into a collaborating whole. Also, drawing the organization's actions into a close fit with the needs of its environment is an essential outcome of the process. This orientation emphasizes that between senders and receivers, the communication process must penetrate social class differences, cultural values, time orientations, and ethnocentrism of all types.

None of the conceptual frameworks, by itself, escapes the barriers to communication. The story of the plumber illustrates the problems of message coding, decoding, and transmission. It is suggested that in order for communication to be effective, an adaptation of the process to the situation should be sought.

When communicating with the outside community, a more structured process may be appropriate, while when communicating with the inside community a less structured process might be more appropriate. This approach is in concert with one of the underlying themes of this book, that, whether speaking about organizational structure, leadership, motivation, or communication, there is a need to adapt the approach or model to the situation. Taking a minute each day to obtain feedback regarding the effectiveness of the communication process at an institution is time well spent and will go a long way to ensuring a healthy organizational environment.

IMPLICATIONS FOR PRACTICE: RELEVANCE OF COMMUNICATION CASE STUDY

Dr. Karen Muda, a newly hired principal, is clearly a strong leader who sees the need for change. She brings a great deal of experience from a former job in which she institutionalized change, and she wants to have it happen again. However, the teachers are not clear as to what needs to be changed, what Dr. Muda's vision for them is, or how the institutionalization will affect them. Because Dr. Muda operates within a situational leadership style, she has confused and frustrated members of the faculty and is quickly setting up divisions within a faculty that had previously been united.

Her recent autocratic decisions regarding detentions have angered teachers, who in the past had been left alone to make those decisions. She has lengthened enormously and completely revamped the structure of monthly faculty meetings. Now the staff is engaged in monthly in-servicing that seems to address Dr. Muda's perceived ineffectualness of the faculty.

The Vroom-Yetton model of the decision-making process describes a stage in which the leader gathers information from subordinates, but does not necessarily tell them what the problem is, and then generates solutions in isolation. Dr. Muda favors engaging in this mode of decision-making. To gather data, individual principal-teacher conferences were held shortly after the start of the school year. She believes these half-hour conferences provided enough information to be acted upon without teachers ever knowing the intention or purpose of these meetings.

As of this date, there has been no forum for teachers to learn of her vision or for her to incorporate subordinates in the decision-making process. Many faculty members, if honest with themselves, would agree there is a need for change, but they are not being given a chance to use their abilities to advance that change. There are many strong, able, experienced "leaders" within the faculty who could initiate change in a positive manner.

Still, Dr. Muda is quickly alienating the staff with her style of leadership in many areas. The staff remains unsure of her direction for change, and the cost of her vision seems to be the loss of some of the staff's innate needs being met. She has taken away their agency, power, and freedom, which had provided them with an internal locus of control under previous administration.

Dr. Muda understands her vision must become their vision in order for institutionalize change to be successful. Communication, like all aspects of leadership, should be contingent on the situation. Regrettably, in this situation, open communication is absent.

DIAGNOSTIC DEBRIEF

Here are some questions that may help in assessing an institution's communication process:

- How effective is the communication process?
- What barriers to communication exist?
- Is the correct communication style utilized under the proper conditions?
- Does communication include feedback, where appropriate?
- Is there a climate of mutual trust and respect?
- Are active listening and other techniques that improve the communication process used?
- Do individuals use assertive, nonassertive, or aggressive communication?

Chapter 6

Decision-making Process

The fine art of executive decision-making consists in not deciding questions that are not now pertinent, in not deciding prematurely, in not making decisions that cannot be made effective, and in not making decisions that others should make.

—*Chester I. Barnard*

Suppose Layla Abbas was appointed to the position of Superintendent of Schools for the Spruce Tree School District with the expressed purpose of rightsizing the school district in light of its declining student population. Having been successful in a similar situation in another school district, how should Layla Abbas proceed?

There are two aspects that Layla must immediately bring to the forefront in the decision-making process, namely the decision's *quality* and its *acceptance*. A high-quality decision brings about the desired result while meeting relevant criteria and constraints. What would constitute a high-quality decision in the situation in Spruce Tree School District? Certainly, a decision that reduces costs while maintaining educational quality would be considered a high-quality one. Also, a decision that met the needs of those affected by the decision, including students, faculty, staff, administrators, and the tax payers would qualify; so too would a decision that meets the financial, human, time, and other constraints existing in the situation.

The quality of the decision depends in part on the level of the decision maker's technical or task skills, interpersonal or leadership skills, and decision-making skills. Technical or task skills refer to the individual's knowledge of the particular area in which the decision is being made. In the decision that Layla Abbas must make about rightsizing, task skills refer to a knowledge of labor costs, projected revenues, educational product information, school system overhead costs, and past experience. Interpersonal or leadership skills relate to the way individuals lead, communicate with, motivate, and influence others. Layla Abbas, for example, must be able convince the other stakeholders in the school system to accept the decision for which she is responsible.

Layla Abbas and any advisors she involves in the decision-making process must produce a decision that they and the rest of the school system community can accept, one that they are willing to "live with." For example, closing two of the schools may be a high-quality decision, but the teachers' union may oppose it so vehemently that the decision may be inoperable. Alternatively, reducing the teaching staff and increasing class size may be a high-quality decision, but parents might resist the change because they feel that their children are not receiving a quality education. Thus, "acceptance" of the decision by the stakeholders is a characteristic that needs to be considered along with the "quality" of the decision.

VROOM/YETTON DECISION-MAKING MODEL

Administrative and organization theory literature agrees about the two most important factors to be considered in determining the decision style which will produce the most effective decisions. While Vroom and Yetton's model includes the additional dimensions of shared goals and conflict possibility, the two key elements are the "quality" and the "acceptance" of the decision, as described earlier. Figure 6.1 summarizes the identification of the decision style which is most appropriate for particular problem types (Vroom and Yetton, 1988).

The two key elements are "quality," or the likelihood of one decision to be more rational and right than another, and "acceptance," or the extent to which acceptance or commitment on the part of stakeholders is crucial to the effective implementation of the decision.

For example, if a new law is passed regarding the education of students with disabilities and the administrator has to decide how to communicate this to the school community, the quality of the decision would be more important than its acceptance. Therefore, the appropriate decision style is "command." On the other hand, if acceptance is more important than quality, as in the development of a new teacher evaluation instrument, the proper decision style would be "consensus."

If both the quality and acceptance are of equal importance, like whether to adopt a whole-language approach to reading instruction, consultation or group decision-making would be the appropriate style. Finally, if neither the quality nor the acceptance is important, like deciding what color to paint the inside of the school closets, convenience would be the applicable style.

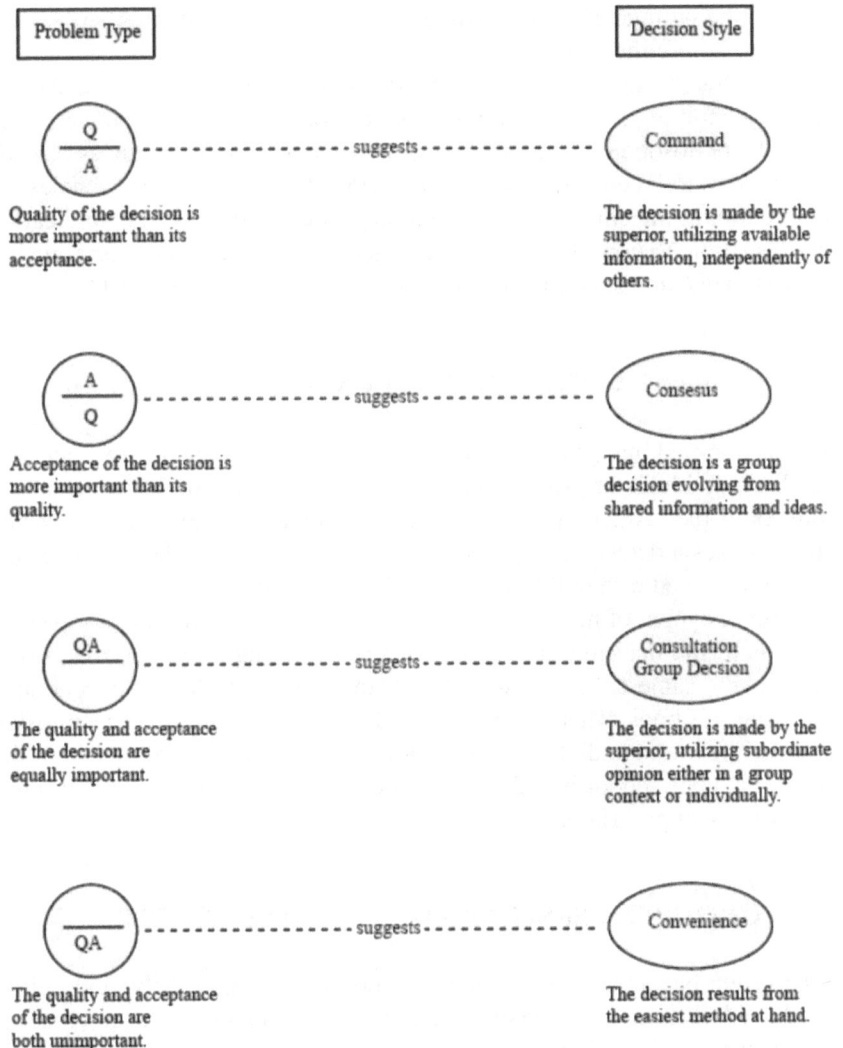

Figure 6.1 The Dimensions of Effective Decisions.

ETHICAL DECISION-MAKING

In addition to evaluating a decision in terms of its quality and acceptance, one can also assess how well it meets the criterion of ethical fairness and justice. Consider, for example, a disastrous decrease in standardized test scores in a certain high school. Top administrators are faced with the decision of whether to risk public outrage and the possible transfer of significant numbers of students or to ignore the situation.

Administrators and staff can assess whether the decisions they make are ethical by applying personal moral codes or society's codes of values; they can apply philosophical views of ethical behavior; or they can assess the potential harmful consequences of behaviors to certain constituencies. A valuable tool in the ethical decision-making process could be the application of the Ignation Vision alluded to in chapter 11, especially the discernment, cura personalis, and social justice aspects of the vision (Rest, 1991).

GROUP DECISION-MAKING

The decision-making processes described thus far can apply to decisions made by individuals or groups. Yet, group decision-making brings different resources to the task situation than does individual decision-making. When a group makes a decision, a synergy occurs that oftentimes causes the group decision to be better than the sum of the individual decisions.

The involvement of more than one individual brings additional knowledge and skills to the decision, and it tends to result in higher quality decisions. However, the same caveat holds for decision-making as has been reiterated throughout this book. That is, decision-making is situational, and the idiosyncrasies of the moment dictate the decision-making approach to be taken. For example, if your school building is on fire, participative decision-making is obviously not appropriate.

GROUP DIVERSITY AND INCLUSIVE PRACTICE

As the group becomes more diverse, attitudinally, behaviorally, and culturally, the advantages of diversity increase. Diversity provides the greatest asset for teams with difficult, discretionary tasks requiring innovation. Still, diversity can be helpful when working on simple tasks involving repetitive and routine procedures. Thus, when establishing a committee or task force to address a complex problem, be certain that its membership reflects the various stakeholders of the school community.

Inclusive practice is a byproduct of group diversity. As a teaching approach, it seeks to recognize differences between students. It then harnesses group diversity to ensure that all participants in the classroom environment can access educational content with full participation in the learning process. Inclusive practice celebrates differences in all people, and, in doing so, influences a decision-making praxis in which learning objectives, instruction, and assessments accommodate individual's diverse needs.

Creating a safe, respectful, trusting, and inclusive group dynamic is a team effort. Despite reflected differences in race, culture, age, religion, sexual orientation, socioeconomic background, and other social identities and life experiences, the goal of inclusiveness, in a diverse community, encourages and appreciates expressions of different ideas, opinions, and beliefs, so that conversations and interactions that could potentially be divisive, turn instead into opportunities for intellectual and personal enrichment.

A dedication to inclusiveness requires respecting what others say, their right to say it, and the thoughtful consideration of others' communication. Both speaking up and listening are valuable tools for furthering thoughtful, enlightening dialogue. Respecting one another's individual differences is critical in transforming a collection of diverse individuals into an inclusive, collaborative, and excellent learning community.

TIME REQUIRED

Group decision-making generally takes more time than individual decision-making. The exchange of information among many individuals, as well as effort spent on obtaining consensus, is time consuming. Sometimes, to reach a decision more quickly or to reach a decision that all group members will accept, groups "satisfice" rather than optimize. That is, they tend to make decisions that are expedient (Simon, 1960).

RISKINESS OF DECISIONS

There is much research to suggest that groups tend to make riskier decisions. Because no single person shoulders the consequences of the decision made by a group, individuals may feel less accountable and will accept more risky or extreme solutions. When a problem occurs in a school, the parents do not complain to the committee, they complain to the principal. Thus, a committee feels free to make a decision that is riskier.

GROUPTHINK

Irving Janis first identified groupthink as a factor that influenced the misguided 1961 Bay of Pigs invasion. The symptoms of groupthink arise when members of decision-making groups try to avoid being too critical in their judgment of other group members' ideas and focus too heavily on developing concurrence. It occurs most frequently in highly cohesive groups, particularly in stressful situations.

Group members experiencing groupthink may feel invulnerable to criticism and hence believe that any action they take or decision they make will be positively received. They may also ignore external criticism, choosing instead to rationalize their actions or decisions as optimum. Some group members may also pressure other group members to agree with the group's decision; deviant opinions are either ignored or not tolerated; members can neither question views offered nor offer disconfirming information. All of these aspects were present in the Bay of Pigs decision (Gordon, 1993).

The Bay of Pigs decision can be contrasted with John F. Kennedy's Cuban Missile Crisis decision that was made of few years later. In this case, Kennedy learned from the Bay of Pigs mistake and did not allow group think to influence the decision-making process, thus yielding dramatically different results.

CHOOSING GROUP DECISION-MAKING

The rule of thumb regarding the use of group decision-making is that unless the "acceptance" of the decision is irrelevant, some type of group decision-making process should be used. Group decision-making is superior when a task or problem requires a variety of expertise, when problems have multiple parts that can be addressed by a division of labor, and when problems require estimates. Individual decision-making results in more efficiency if policy dictates the correct solution.

Individual decision-making also tends to lead to more effective decisions for problems that require completion of a series of complex stages, so long as the individual receives input from many sources, because it allows better coordination of the phases in solving the problem. In Spruce Tree School District, for example, the main decision that Layla Abbas and her colleagues must make is how to reduce costs without reducing quality. This type of problem requires diverse knowledge and skills, creativity, and completion of a series of complex stages, calling most likely for a combination of individual and group decision-making.

Group decision-making more often leads to acceptance than does decision-making by individuals. In addition, since individuals involved in making a decision generally become committed to the decision, use of group consensus expedites acceptance of the decision by the group, thereby increasing individual and group commitment to the decision. Acceptance of the decision about rightsizing at Spruce Tree may affect its implementation in the short run, and since school employees cannot easily be replaced, may also affect it in the long run. Therefore, the acceptance is as important as the quality of the decision.

Group decision-making generally leads to higher quality solutions unless an individual's expertise in the decision areas is identified in the beginning. At Spruce Tree, Layla Abbas has had successful experience in rightsizing; therefore, she has less need for group input to make a high-quality decision. However, she needs the input because the acceptance of the decision is so important.

The amount of time available will determine whether group problem-solving is feasible because group decision-making takes much more time than individual decision-making. Spruce Tree School District must resolve its problem in a timely manner or risk a taxpayer revolt; therefore, the amount of group participation may be somewhat limited.

WAYS TO IMPROVE DECISION-MAKING

How can decision makers overcome barriers, reduce biases, and make more effective decisions? There are at least three techniques that can improve decision-making: brainstorming, the nominal group technique, and the Delphi technique.

Brainstorming

Groups or individuals use brainstorming when creativity is needed to generate many alternatives for consideration in decision-making. In brainstorming, they list as many alternatives as possible without simultaneously evaluating the feasibility of any alternative. For example, Layla Abbas might charge a task force with listing all the ways of reducing costs in the Spruce Tree School District. The absence of evaluation encourages group members to generate rather than defend ideas. Then, after ideas have been generated, they are evaluated and decisions are made. Although brainstorming can result in many shallow and useless ideas, it can also motivate members to offer new ideas. It works best when individuals have a common view of what constitutes a good idea, but it is harder to use when specialized knowledge or complex implementation is required (Adams, 1986).

Nominal Group Technique

The nominal group technique is a structured group meeting that helps resolve differences in group opinion by having individuals generate and then rank order a series of ideas in the problem: exploration, alternative generation, or choice-making stages of the process (Michaelson, 1989). A group of individuals is presented with a stated problem. Each person individually offers alternative solutions in writing. The group then shares the solutions and lists them on a blackboard or large piece of paper, as in brainstorming. The group discusses and clarifies the ideas. They then rank and vote their preference for the various ideas. If the group has not reached an agreement, they repeat the ranking and voting procedure until the group reaches some agreement.

Nominal group technique encourages innovation, limits conflict, emphasizes equal participation by all members, helps generate consensus, and incorporates the preferences of individuals in decision-making choices. However, unless the administrator is trained in the use of this technique and the ones that follow, it would be more prudent to employ an organizational consultant who is trained and has experience in these techniques to act as a facilitator in the process. Figure 6.2 illustrates the steps in nominal group technique.

Delphi Technique

Basically, the Delphi technique structures group communication in dealing with a complex problem in four phases: exploration of the subject by individuals, reaching understanding of the group's view of the issues, sharing and evaluation of any reasons for differences, and final evaluation of all information. In the conventional Delphi, a small group designs a questionnaire, which is completed by a larger respondent group; the results are then tabulated and used in developing a revised questionnaire, which is again completed by the larger group. Thus, the results of the original polling are fed back to the respondent group to use in subsequent responses. This procedure is repeated until the issues are narrowed, responses are focused, or consensus is reached (Huber, 75).

Delphi is very helpful in a variety of circumstances.

- First, if the decision makers cannot apply precise analytical techniques to solving the problem but prefer to use subjective judgments on a collective basis, Delphi can provide input from a large number of respondents.
- Second, if the individuals involved have historically failed to communicate effectively in the past, the Delphi procedures offer a systematic method for ensuring that all opinions are presented.
- Third, the Delphi does not require face-to-face interaction and thus succeeds when the group is too large for such a direct exchange.

Decision-making Process

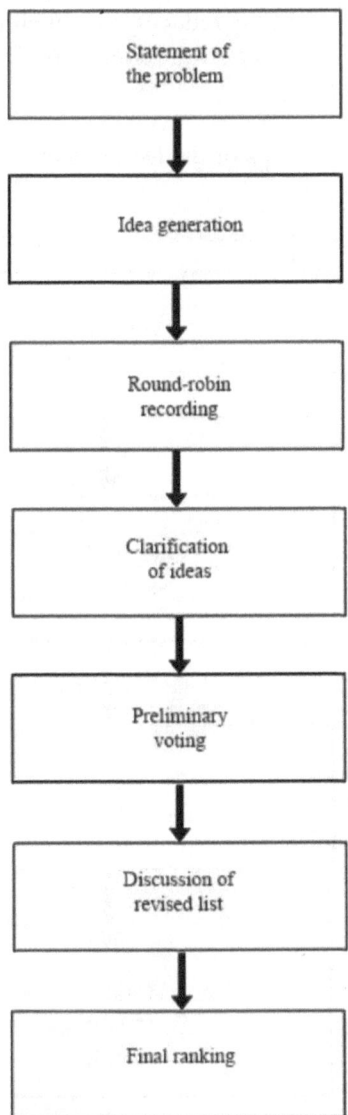

Figure 6.2 Steps in Nominal Grouping.

- Fourth, when time and cost prevent frequent group meetings or when a pre-meeting communication would be helpful, the Delphi technique offers significant value for decision-making.
- Fifth, the Delphi can also overcome situations where individuals greatly disagree or where the anonymity of views must be maintained to protect group members.

- Finally, the Delphi technique reduces the likelihood of groupthink; it prevents one or more members from dominating by their numbers or the strength of their personality.

Figure 6.3 summarizes the steps of the Delphi technique.

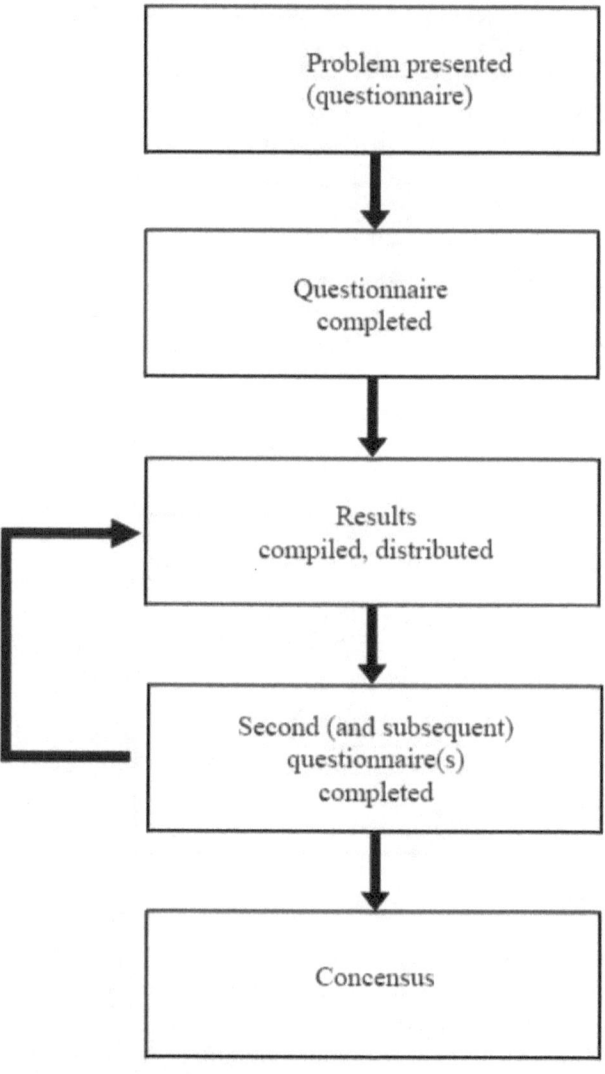

Figure 6.3 Steps in the Delphi Technique.

CONCLUSION

Decision-making is a basic and important process in educational institutions. The success experienced by educational administrators depends largely on their mastery and effective implementation of the decision-making process. This chapter describes the nature of the decision being made in rightsizing the Spruce Tree School District.

It is noted that to make such decisions effective individuals must have technical, interpersonal, and decision-making skills. Outlined are basic decision-making processes that help improve the quality of a decision and encourage its acceptance by others. Furthermore, quality and acceptance are the two most important factors to be considered in rendering a decision. Decision makers must systematically analyze the situation; set objectives; generate, evaluate, and select alternatives; make the decision; and evaluate the decision made.

This process stresses the situational nature of effective decision-making. There is no one singular decision-making style that is effective at all times and in all situations. In response, some techniques to improve decision-making, including the nominal group technique, brainstorming, and the Delphi technique, are recommended. Taking a few minutes each day to determine what decision-making model is best for a given situation is another vital step leading to effective administration.

IMPLICATIONS FOR PRACTICE: DECISION-MAKING MODELS CASE STUDY

Hillside Middle School is an inner-city public school with 403 students enrolled. In total, 83 percent of the students are African American, 9 percent are of Latinx descent, 6 percent are Caucasian, and the remaining 2 percent are Asian; 98 percent of the students are enrolled in a reduced meal program. Students are largely from the local area, living in high density apartment complexes, subsidized public housing, as well as private homes, and a number of them reside as permanent residents in area shelters.

Hillside Middle School is in the Woodfield School District, the largest district in the state. The superintendent of the district, Dr. Rylan Newell, has been with the district for two years. Dr. Newell's innovative improvement program, called *Children to Achieve*, is a plan based in the belief that all children can learn and should have every opportunity to do so.

Dr. Newell wants students to become active participants in the learning process; therefore, it supports a student-centered mode of teaching. Dr. Newell has implemented "standards" into the curriculum, a series of outcomes students must meet before graduating or before being promoted to the next grade level. The facilitation of the teacher is crucial in order for students to meet the requirements necessary in relation to the standard. Dr. Newell also believes that the teacher should be held accountable for student achievement.

Accountability has set the tone for many schools in the district. Schools like Hillside are reevaluating the way in which they implement and teach their curriculum. Before Dr. Newell revealed a student-centered agenda, Hillside administrators took a "hands-off" approach to universal curriculum implementation. Each teacher had their own style, plan, and set of goals for classroom instruction. Teaching strategies varied from classroom to classroom, teacher to teacher. The principal's theory was simple: If your class is quiet and students are working on something, "Hillside is doing its job as a school!"

All of this was about to change though, with the unveiling of Dr. Newell's *Children to Achieve* plan. Of utmost consideration for Dr. Newell is the best implementation approach for her plan (*unconscious bias check—did you imagine Dr. Newell to be a man, if so, ask yourself why*), especially for schools with unique challenges and opportunities, like Hillside Middle School.

DIAGNOSTIC DEBRIEF

Here are some questions that may be helpful in assessing the decision-making process in an institution:

- Do organizational members make high-quality, accepted, and ethical decisions?
- Do decision makers follow a rational process of decision-making?
- Is the group appropriately involved in decision-making?
- Are techniques such as brainstorming, nominal group, and the Delta techniques being used to facilitate the decision-making process?

Chapter 7

Conflict Management Process

If we manage conflict constructively, we harness its energy for creativity and development.

—Kenneth Kaye

Some may argue the need to be right is what really matters; however, being heard (whether right or wrong) may be equally or in many cases even more important. Conflict is the result of incongruent or incompatible relationships between and within individuals, groups, or organizations. Conflict can be public or private, formal or informal, rational or non-rational. The likelihood of conflict increases when parties have the chance to interact, when the parties see their differences as incompatible, and when there is a power differential between the parties that results in the dependence of one party on the other.

Conflict most commonly results in four circumstances. First, when mutually exclusive goals or values actually exist or are perceived to exist by the groups involved, conflict can occur. In the collective bargaining process, for example, the teachers' union may perceive that the administration's goals may be incompatible with those of the teachers, and vice versa.

Another circumstance of conflict is when behavior is designed to defeat, reduce, or suppress the opponent. An example of this type of conflict often takes place in labor relations work. Specifically, union and management have historically experienced conflict for this reason.

A symbiotic relationship based on interdependence is a third circumstance of conflict. This takes place when individuals or groups are dependent on one another. For example, if the second-grade teacher does not follow the curriculum, the third-grade teacher will be affected because the students will not have been properly prepared. In this example, it remains understandable how the third-grade teacher might feel disenfranchised by the lack of student learning and skill development based on the negligent actions of the second-grade instructor.

The last conflict circumstance commonly occurs when each group attempts to create a relatively favored position. If the English department attempts to show administration that it is superior to the other departments by demonstrating the others' ineptness, conflict occurs. Knowing these sources of conflict can go a long way toward precluding the surfacing of conflicts in the first place. A little preventative medicine, so to speak, is always in order.

Conflict can have functional or dysfunctional outcomes. Effective administrators learn how to create functional conflict, prevent conflict from arising, and manage dysfunctional conflict when it does occur. They develop and practice techniques for diagnosing the causes and nature of conflict and transforming it into a productive force in the organization. Many colleges, for example, have a healthy competition between and among schools within the university for the recruitment of the most qualified students.

Some conflict is beneficial. It can encourage organizational change in the form of innovation, creativity, and adaption. For example, a number of non-public school systems, and even some public school systems, allow schools within the system to compete for the same students. This "open enrollment" policy often spawns innovation in marketing techniques, and more importantly, in curriculum and instruction.

Interestingly, conflict can be viewed as dysfunctional for organizations. It can reduce productivity, decrease morale, cause overwhelming dissatisfaction, and increase tension and stress in the organization. It can arouse anxiety in individuals, increase the tension in an organizational system and its subsystems, and lower satisfaction levels. Production and satisfaction may decline; turnover and absenteeism may increase.

Administrators have at least five behaviors or strategies for dealing with conflict: avoidance, accommodation, compromise, competing/forcing, and collaborating. Each style is appropriate to different situations that individuals or groups face in organizations. Once again, the underlying theme of contingency theory applies. These behaviors are illustrated in table 7.1.

Avoidance

Individuals or groups may withdraw from the conflict situation. They act to satisfy neither their own or the other party's concerns. Avoidance works best when individuals or groups face trivial or tangential tissues, when they have little chance of satisfying their personal concerns, when

Table 7.1 Five Conflict Modes.

Conflict Handling Modes	Appropriate Situations
Competing	1. When quick, decisive action is vital—e.g., emergencies 2. On important issues where unpopular actions need implementing—e.g., cost cutting, enforcing unpopular rules, discipline 3. On issues vital to institutional welfare when you know you are right
Collaborating	1. To find an integrative solution when both sets of concerns are too important to be compromised 2. When your objective is to learn 3. To merge insights from people with different perspectives 4. To gain commitment by incorporating concerns into a consensus 5. To work through feelings that have interfered with a relationship
Compromising	1. When goals are important but not worth the effort or potential disruption of more assertive modes 2. When opponents with equal power are committed to mutually exclusive goals 3. To achieve temporary settlements to complex issues 4. To arrive at expedient solutions under time pressure
Avoiding	1. When an issue is trivial or more important issues are pressing 2. When you perceive no chance of satisfying your concerns 3. When potential disruption outweighs the benefits of resolution 4. To let people cool down and regain perspective 5. When gathering information supersedes immediate decision
Accommodating	1. When you find you are wrong—to allow a better position to be heard, to learn, and to show your reasonableness 2. When issues are more important to others than yourself—to satisfy others and maintain cooperation 3. To build social credits for later issues 4. To minimize loss when you are outmatched and losing 5. When harmony and stability are especially important

conflict resolution will likely result in significant disruption, or when others can resolve the conflict more effectively. If two secretaries in the secretarial pool, for example, have an argument, the most appropriate strategy for managing the conflict may be avoidance. Let the secretaries resolve the conflict in their own ways.

In some circumstances avoidance might be the right choice to management conflict. Consider the proverbial story of the next-door neighbors whose children got into an argument and the adults tried to intervene on behalf of their respective children. The adults ended up being lifelong enemies and the children were playing with each other again within the hour.

ACCOMMODATION

Individuals or groups who use accommodation, sometimes called diffusion, demonstrate willingness to cooperate in satisfying others' concerns, while at the same time acting unassertively in meeting their own. Accommodating individuals often smooth over conflict. This mode builds social capital for later issues, results in harmony and stability, and satisfies others. An assistant principal may capitulate on a disagreement with the principal over a minor matter in hopes that he or she can prevail on a larger issue in the future, thus building political and social capital to be used later. Again, accommodation can be an example of the age-old adage of losing the battle, but winning the war.

COMPROMISE

The compromise mode represents an intermediate behavior. It can include a sharing of positions, but not moving to the extremes. Hence, it often does not maximize satisfaction of both parties. This style works well when goals are important but not sufficiently important for the individual or group to be more assertive, when the two parties have equal power, or when significant time pressure exists. For example, if two grade partners disagree over what supplementary materials should be used for a certain lesson, they may compromise and use some of each teacher's suggestions.

COMPETING/FORCING

In competing or forcing mode, one party tries to satisfy its own concerns while showing an unwillingness to satisfy the other's concerns to even a minimal degree. This strategy works well in emergencies, on issues calling for unpopular actions, and in cases where one party is correct in its position or where one party has much greater power. For example, if a child tries to commit suicide, the principal may wish to inform the parents immediately and the guidance counselor may wish it to remain confidential. If the principal arbitrarily informs the parents immediately, he or she is using competing/forcing behavior.

COLLABORATING

The collaboration mode emphasizes problem-solving with a goal of maximizing satisfaction for both parties, often resulting in a win/win solution. It means seeing conflict as natural, showing trust and honesty toward others, and encouraging the airing of every person's attitudes and feelings. Each party exerts both assertive and cooperative behavior. Parties can use it when their objectives are to learn, to use information from diverse sources, and to find an integrative solution. If the teacher's union and the school board agree to consider their differences to be "our" problems rather than "your" problems, they are taking a collaborative or problem-solving approach to resolve or avoid conflict.

One effective approach is, once one decides that avoidance is not appropriate; begin efforts toward conflict resolution with the collaborative mode. If that is not successful, move progressively to compromise and accommodation, using forcing only as a last resort. And keep mindful to consider the role and interplay of both explicit and implicit bias (see chapter 2 for definitions of these terms) in collaborative processes.

IMPLICATIONS FOR PRACTICE: CONFLICT MANAGEMENT PROCESS CASE STUDY

Hawthorne High School (HHS) is situated in a solidly upper-middle-class community. It has a strong tax base and a population that is very concerned with the quality of education provided by public schools. Parental involvement in ancillary school functions frequently leads to parental influence on academic matters. Consequently, the school relinquishes its prerogative as purveyor of the curriculum.

Despite ample opportunities and resources to support learning, school discipline is the area of professional responsibility where Hawthorne is most derelict. Codified school district procedures are ignored in favor of a laissez-faire approach, permitting a myriad of inappropriate behaviors. Attempts to gain control of the learning environment lead to parental complaints. Parental complaints are given forum by an extremely political administration that disenfranchises the teaching staff. The general population of students at Hawthorne experience school as low risk for consequences when involved in unruly disciplinary behaviors.

During one spring, necessary equipment, materials, and machinery for several upcoming summer renovation projects were being staged in a school parking lot. The area was sectioned off with yellow caution tape to prevent access and to ensure student safety. There were also aides assigned to supervise this area before and after school (despite countless discussions concerning the effectiveness of the aides' supervision).

Despite many factors contributing to these discussions, the aides were not trained in effective management control and they do not believe they have control (which student can sense immediately). Even though the aides go through school district in-service, they hold no power for following through on disciplinary actions. Past experiences document the aides and students screaming at each other.

Students file formal complaints expressing their frustrations, blaming the aides. Rather than believing the school employee, who has no motive to fabricate stories of misbehavior, parents overwhelmingly support their children and blame the aides as well. Parents claim the aides capriciously yell at their student.

One day twenty-five to thirty seniors were on a tear. They were jumping on top of one another, causing classmates to fall to the ground. Their behavior was creating a safety hazard. They had broken through the caution tape from the construction site and were wrapping the brightly colored plastic around their necks and waists. What was even more appalling was that the aides were standing right there not taking command.

The next day, HHS principal, James Cannon, was seen verbally reprimanding the aides before the start of classes because the aides "couldn't handle it." He also threatened to fire the entire team of aides. Later that day, Mr. Cannon met with teacher leaders to brainstorm ideas on how to handle this situation.

Mrs. Parsons, a teacher for over twenty years, suggested nonnegotiable after-school detention for all students involved. Mr. Cannon would not agree with that option, fearing even more complaints. Furthermore, he characterized this suggestion as a punishment. He then began to explain how imposing consequences of this nature are not allowable, as Dr. Donna Ricci, the district superintendent, does not support group punishment.

Principal Cannon was not only unsupportive of other suggestions but also took away teacher agency and authority. What Dr. Ricci and Mr. Cannon refer to as group punishment is what many teacher leaders consider crisis management.

In the end, no solution was found, and the teacher leaders were frustrated because input was requested but not considered. Students involved in the incident were not disciplined, had no repercussion, and aides' professional credibility was undermined by the administration. Throughout the remainder of the spring, students continued to be disrespectful and the aides still lacked control.

DIAGNOSTIC DEBRIEF

Here are some questions that may help assess the conflict management capabilities of an institution:

- Is the conflict in the institution functional or dysfunctional?
- Are preventative measures being employed to preclude conflict from occurring?
- Are there mechanisms for effectively managing conflict and stress?
- Does the use of these mechanisms reflect the situational nature of conflict resolution?
- Are avoidance, compromise, forcing, accommodation, and collaboration utilized in the appropriate situations?

Chapter 8

Empowerment for Success

You must never be fearful about what you are doing when it is right.

—Rosa Parks

Power is the potential or actual ability to influence others in a desired direction. Who has the power in a situation? An individual, group, or other social unit has power if it controls information, knowledge, or resources desired by another individual, group, or social unit. Do different types of power exist? If so, which type is more effective in organization leadership?

In this chapter, power and the negotiations process are examined. The chapter begins by considering the reasons individuals or groups exert power. Then, the text examines the sources from which one derives power. Next, the collective bargaining process is explained. Specifically, two bargaining paradigms, the negotiation process, and some of the strategies and tactics used in negotiations are described.

POWER IN THE ORGANIZATION

Organizational researchers have increasingly cited the value of identifying and using power behavior to improve individual and organizational performance, even calling its development and use "the central executive function" (Kotter, 1986). Theorists and practitioners have transformed an early view of power, which considered it evil and as mainly stemming from coercion, into a model of viable political action in organizations. Yet, although functional and advantageous in many situations, power behavior can also create conflict, which frequently is dysfunctional for the organization (Kaplan, 1964).

ETHICAL ISSUES

How legitimate is the use of power in organizations? Certainly, if the use of power is manipulative and autocratic, it raises questions about the ethics of power. The abuse of power is evident not only in politics but also in schools, school districts, and institutions of higher education.

Administrators should establish guidelines for the ethical use of power in their institutions. They and other organizational members must emphasize its contribution to organizational effectiveness and control its abuses. Ensuring that the rights of all organizational members are guaranteed is one criterion for its ethical use. This is especially appropriate in institutions that are not unionized, where the faculty and staff handbook should outline employee rights in a way similar to that of a labor agreement. Chapter 11 spoke of developing covenants or informal agreements between employees and management.

POWER AND DEPENDENCE

We can initially diagnose the level of power someone has by estimating the extent of the dependence that flows in the opposite direction from power in a relationship (Kotter, 1977). In other words, the power that Charlotte Burton has over Marie Wilson is determined by the degree of dependence that Marie Wilson has on Charlotte Burton.

Dependence arises in part because a person, group, or organization relies on another person, group, or organization to accomplish his, her, or its tasks. A subordinate depends on his or her ordinates for assistance in accomplishing a task and identifying obstacles to achieving a work goal. The person being relied or depended upon automatically has some power to influence the other.

Marie Wilson, for example, might attempt to have the untenured teachers believe that their continued employment depends largely on her support as a way to increase their dependence on her. On the other hand, Charlotte Burton might circumvent Marie Wilson as much as possible to display her independence from union influence and demonstrate to the teachers that their future employment depends more on Charlotte Burton than on Marie Wilson.

EMPOWERING OTHERS

In a site-based or school-based management situation, for example, superintendents and principals are relinquishing some of their power. Task forces, whose membership reflects the makeup of the school community, are given either advisory or governance power in making decisions. This process empowers faculty and staff but ultimately enhances the power of the administration, because the school is more likely to achieve its goals—and if it does, the administration looks good which, if effect, increases its power.

SOURCES OF POWER

Albeit there are different ways of grouping or organizing sources of power. The preferred strategy consists of two larger categories: organizational and personal power. Under each of these categories are specific types of power.

Organizational Power

Organizational power is a broad category used to describe one's ability to influence the behavior of others within the organization. The measurement of power is determined by the extension of influence one has to get another stakeholder to comply with a request that the stakeholder might otherwise not wish to do. Legitimate, reward, and coercive power fall under organizational power.

Leaders who possess *legitimate* or *position power* (as it is also referred) can exert influence over others simply because of the authority associated with their job. It results in subordinates obeying the instructions given by a principal, for example, simply by virtue of the position that he or she holds. In education, the union contract and tenure mitigate the principal's legitimate power to a significant degree. Thus, it is inappropriate to rely on position as the only source of power. One study showed, for example, that as a supervisor's position power increased, a subordinate's compliance increased, but his or her satisfaction with supervision decreased (Rahim, 1989). So, in the long run, the abuse of legitimate power can have diminishing returns.

Reward power (sometimes called *resource power*) is based on the notion that someone has control over resources or rewards others within the organization want. Initially, reward power may be viewed with positive regard; however, the ability to withhold the reward for noncompliance is also a feature of this power type. Consider the senior financial administrator within the school district. Their ability to control the allocation of fiscal resources may provide reward power for those who seek funding for special projects or interests.

Power can come from the control of scarce resources, such as money, materials, staff, or information. In a school setting, the business manager oftentimes has this type of power. Even information technology and communication personnel can have this type of power if there is a greater demand than there is a supply of these types of resources in an organization.

Harnessing *coercive power* means successfully motivating others by fear. Within the 2006 film, *The Devil Wears Prada*, one of the main characters, Miranda Priestly, is depicted as a diabolical editor for a global fashion magazine. Miranda exerts coercive power which influences subordinates to either cower when in her presence or causes them to run in the opposite direction to avoid being in the same space as she. Coercive power can be very damaging in a workplace setting and has been linked to long-term traumatic stress for many who fall victim to its use.

Important for consideration is also the centrality of power. Specifically, power accrues to other positions because of their centrality. The more the activities of a position are linked and important to those of other individuals or subunits, the greater their centrality. A superintendent of schools, for example, has greater centrality than the school board because the activities of more jobs are linked to him or her than to the elected school board. Thus, even though the school board technically has more reward power, in reality, the superintendent has more legitimate power because of the centrality of their position.

Personal Power

Personal power is based on the knowledge or personality of an individual that allows them to influence the behavior of others. There are two power types categorized under personal power: expert and referent power.

An individual who has unique or special knowledge, skills, and experience can use this expertise as a source of influence and as a way of building personal power. For example, when new innovative technology or learning devices are introduced into the market, the "techie" on the faculty oftentimes wields personal power based on their special knowledge and skills. In this scenario, e*xert power* allows the IT savvy faculty member to have influence over others.

As schools and other organizations have become increasingly technology-oriented, many technical support staff have acquired increased expert power within their organization. Admittedly, everyone has a "super power," a specialized skill and/or area of knowledge, where they may be deemed an expert by peers. The goal is to harness this expertise to impact the way others think or behave.

There are some people who just have an electric aura, commanding presence, and a contagious personality. These individuals influence others because they have charisma or because others identify closely with shared values, beliefs, thoughts, or behaviors. This is called *referent power*.

An individual with charisma often exerts power because they attract others to follow. It is important to distinguish that under this power type, others want to be associated with a specific individual; the inclination for following a command or order is completely voluntary and not based on positional power. Oftentimes, when lateral dependence occurs among peers, it is the result of referent power based on an individual's charisma.

As previously mentioned, access to resources or information provides a source of influence under reward power. Another source of power often associated with reward power, but with less transience is expertise. Expertise is more permanent than information-based power. For example, the first individuals to learn to use a new computer application/software might initially derive their power from having information that others do not, but if their power persists even after the average teacher becomes digitally literate, personal power based on expertise has been obtained. Understandably, expert power is strongly associated with high performance and skill development.

THE NEGOTIATIONS PROCESS

In the field of education, perhaps the prototypical display of power occurs most often through the negotiations or collective bargaining process. In other words, negotiation is a tactical response and extension of power. Negotiation is a process by which two or more parties attempt to reach an agreement that is acceptable to both parties about issues on which they disagree.

Negotiations typically have four key elements (Lax and Sebenius, 1986). First, the two parties demonstrate some degree of interdependence. Charlotte Burton and Marie Wilson demonstrate such interdependence. Second, some perceived conflict exists between the parties involved in the negotiations. Ordinarily, the teachers' union and the school administration differ in their views on exactly how the school should operate. Third, the two parties have the potential to participate in opportunistic interaction. Therefore, each party tries to influence the other through various negotiating actions. Each party cares about and pursues its own interests, by trying to influence decisions to its advantage. Finally, the possibility of agreement or settlement exists.

BARGAINING PARADIGMS

Basically, two bargaining paradigms are in current use: distributive bargaining, which takes an adversarial or win-lose approach, and integrative bargaining, which takes a problem-solving or win-win approach.

The classical view considers bargaining as a win-lose situation, where one party's gain is the other party's loss. Known also as a zero-sum type of negotiation, because the gain of one party equals the loss of the other and hence the net adds to zero, this approach characterizes the great majority of the negotiations taking place in educational settings today.

Recent research encourages negotiators to transform the bargaining into a win-win situation. Here, both parties gain as a result of the negotiations. Known also as a positive-sum type of negotiation, because the gains of each party yield a positive sum, this approach has recently characterized the negotiations in a few school districts, especially those that have had a history of strikes and are looking for an alternative to the classical model of collective bargaining.

DISTRIBUTIVE BARGAINING

Even when an agreement is reached, distributive bargaining tends to lead to a win-lose conclusion between the parties. Both parties tend to depict the other as the loser to their respective constituencies. When the negotiations break down into a serious impasse, the probability of a lose/lose outcome increases. In this circumstance, not only are the parties frustrated from achieving a satisfactory agreement, but those whom they serve are affected adversely. The teaching-learning environment can be disrupted by the hostility between the parties. Parents, students, and the community in general can become angry when the school is unable to function properly because of unsettled disputes between the school's management and its employees (Fisher and Ury, 1981).

INTEGRATIVE/COLLABORATIVE BARGAINING

An alternative form of bargaining has emerged as a way to avoid or minimize the negative aspects of adversarial bargaining. Collaborative bargaining represents a cooperative process that focuses on problem-solving and other activities that identify, enlarge, and act upon the common interests of the parties. Its objective is to increase the joint gain of the parties, the win-win outcome.

The pressure for educational reform in the last two decades has stimulated teachers and school boards to negotiate collaboratively over policy issues dealing with class size, staff development, student achievement on standardized tests, and teacher appraisal methods. Collaborative bargaining is a timely method for joining the general trend of school reforms that seek to institutionalize collaborative decision-making into the daily operations of schools. Collaborative bargaining rests on the assumptions that both parties want to achieve a mutually satisfactory agreement and that the agreement will lead to an improved school environment for students.

Table 8.1 Goldaber's Win-Win Contract Development Program.

Phase	Activity
1	Both sides receive protocols governing the process.
2	Each side lists questions and concerns for phase 3.
WEEKEND ONE	THE COMMUNICATIONS LABORATORY
3	All participants and the facilitator meet.
4	Issues are identified for inclusion in the contract and contract matter committees are appointed.
5	Committees discuss issues, finalize agreements, and list unresolved issues (approximately thirty days allowed).
WEEKEND TWO	CONTRACT DRAFTING
6	All participants and the facilitator meet to reach agreement on the contract.
7	The writing committee drafts the proposed contract.
8	All participants review the proposed contract and recommend its approval to their constituents.
9	Each side votes on the proposed contract.
10	All participants meet to witness the signing on the contract.

An example of an integrative or collaborative bargaining approach is the win-win process developed by Irving Goldaber. In this process, the parties are given a fixed period of time in which to negotiate a contract. In so doing, the parties are to arrive at shared solutions without either being forced to give up its desired goals (Palestini, 2012).

Goldaber's win-win approach is organized into ten phases depicted in table 8.1. The preliminary phases entail each party receiving the protocols for structuring the process and preparing lists of questions, concerns, and expectations. These lists are copied onto large sheets of paper for posting around the room during the first formal meeting of the process.

The third and fourth phases occur during the first two weekends that bound the fixed time period (usually thirty days) for reaching an agreement. This weekend is conducted as a communications laboratory to deal with areas of distrust and to reach the realization that each side needs the other to resolve their conflicts. The questions prepared in phase two provide a way for the parties to communicate and share their concerns with each other.

In its typical structure, the laboratory may begin on a Friday evening and extends through all day Saturday. The participants are representatives of the two parties (an equal number from both sides, plus resource persons they invite) and an external facilitator who conducts the laboratory. The end goal of the laboratory, the fourth phase, is to identify issues for collective bargaining and to appoint contract matter committees.

During the next thirty days, the fifth phase, the contract matter committees meet, discuss, and attempt to reach an agreement on issues to be included in a collective bargaining agreement. One committee might address salary and benefits; a second, working conditions; and a third, rights and responsibilities. A fourth committee might be established to deal with any items not assigned to the other committees. Their job is to finalize agreement on as many items as possible. Unresolved issues are to be listed and brought to the second weekend meeting of the entire group.

Collective bargaining itself takes place during the committee meetings. But rather than following the traditional distributive approach, the parties are urged to seek new and creative solutions to problems. They are also encouraged to concede voluntarily on positions whenever it is possible to do so. Mutual respect and empathy for the greater good of the school should guide the deliberations.

At the end of the fixed period for bargaining, all participants reconvene for a second weekend (phase six). Agreed-upon items are confirmed, and unresolved items are addressed. When success is achieved in reaching agreement on all items, a contract writing committee is appointed to put the agreement in final form. The remaining phases, seven through ten, deal with reviewing and recommending the proposed agreement, formal ratification, and the signing of the contract.

The use of the Goldaber model has been more successful in affecting attitudes than the content of the agreements. The model has had an astounding success rate, with management and employees citing a freer, more open exchange and the problem-solving approach promoted greater awareness of the other side's point of view on issues.

One of the drawbacks to the process outlined in the Goldaber model is that both managements' and employees' constituencies may be locked into the distributive paradigm of negotiations. There is a tendency to think that the best-possible agreement has not been achieved because negotiations do not necessarily continue until Labor Day. In order for the process to be effective, then, a great deal of staff development needs to take place before negotiations even begin so that both parties' constituencies have realistic expectations of what the results of the process will be.

EFFECTIVE NEGOTIATIONS

We can identify at least four basic steps in effective negotiation for either distributive or integrative bargaining. First, the parties prepare for the negotiations. Second, they determine the model they will use and develop their bargaining strategies. Third, they negotiate a settlement, and fourth, they administer the agreed-upon contract (Goldaber, 1987).

PRE-NEGOTIATION PREPARATION

The preparation phase of the negotiation process is as important as the negotiations themselves. It is with proper preparation that many problems during the actual negotiations can be precluded. The preparation phase begins the day after the last contract is signed. It continues until the next contract is negotiated, but picks up in intensity about six months before the negotiation sessions begin. One of the first steps in the preparation process is to anticipate the issues that will be negotiated. An effective way of doing this is to review the grievances that have occurred during the administration of the current contract. This review will identify the problematic areas of the present contract and be an accurate indicator of what will most likely be the substance of the upcoming negotiations.

Another step in the preparation process is the gathering of information regarding comparable settlements in other school districts and neighboring institutions of similarity. Data regarding the Consumer Price Index is also important to have. Demographic data regarding the school district, like the average age of the faculty, student enrollment projections, property tax expectations, and budget projections, should be gathered. Finally, the negotiation team should be assembled during this phase.

The makeup of the negotiation team should reflect appropriate segments of the school community. From management's point of view, the team should include representatives from the central office, local school administrators, and a member of the school board. Many times, legal counsel is part of the team and frequently serves as the chief negotiator. It is not advisable for the superintendent or the highest-ranking administrative officer to be on the team because that person needs to remain as the respected leader of the school district after the contract is negotiated and should not be associated too closely with what is too often an adversarial process.

The choice of chief negotiator is the next step in constituting the negotiating team. This person must be knowledgeable of the prevailing collective bargaining laws and the bargaining process itself. The abilities to plan, analyze, and coordinate the activities of the team are essential. Being able to articulate the various positions is also extremely important. The personal qualities of tolerance and persistence are needed to ensure that the process is conducted in a rational, calm manner and is kept on course toward achieving an agreement.

From a practical perspective, team members should be identified according to the expertise needed in the process. One person, generally the chief negotiator, should be a skilled spokesperson. Another member should be a specialist in the wording of proposals; another in cost analysis; another in keeping written records of key discussions; and at least one who knows the current contract provisions thoroughly.

DEVELOPING A BARGAINING STRATEGY

The second phase of the negotiation process is developing the bargaining strategy. This phase includes the mutual decision of whether a distributive or an integrated model is to be used. Once a model is selected, the identification of key issues takes place. Management must determine what goals it plans to achieve as a result of the process. For example, management might wish to hold the line on school governance issues, or hold the line on salary and fringe benefit costs to 1 percent above the cost-of-living increase. Management might wish to rectify a salary inequity between junior and senior faculty or address a class-size issue. Once the broad-based goals are developed, a rationale for each proposal needs to be prepared (Fisher and Brown, 1988).

THE BARGAINING PROCESS

Maintaining an atmosphere of reasonableness and civility during the bargaining process is important if a settlement is to be reached. Certain protocols should be maintained so that common courtesy prevails. Once the proper atmosphere is established, the negotiators can go about their business of presenting, evaluating, and responding to each other's proposals. Once proposals are presented, those that have cost implications need to be identified and "costed out." It is an effective tactic to consider the cost items as a "package," rather than individually.

It is essential that the negotiation team presents a united front. Never disagree on an issue at the bargaining table. If there is disagreement or misunderstanding among members of the team, a private caucus should be called to resolve the differences before returning to the table. In addition, a careful rationale for each proposal should be developed and a reasoned response to the other parties' proposals should be articulated. It is also effective to accept certain of the other parties' proposals as a "trade-off" for the acceptance of one of your own proposals. Finally, when reaching agreement on an issue, be certain that the proper wording is incorporated into the contract because the parties will have to live with it for the duration of the agreement.

When the parties fail to reach a settlement, an impasse may be declared. In the case of many educational institutions, state law determines how an impasse is handled. In general, however, the process may proceed from mediation to fact finding and then to arbitration.

The mediation process is one through which a third party seeks to facilitate the process and resolve the impasse. The objective is to assist the parties to arrive at an agreement of their own creation. The mediator typically meets with each party's negotiating team separately to explain the process and to ascertain each party's view of the disputed issues. Then, in a joint meeting, the mediator summarizes the issues with the effort to ensure that each party's position is understood clearly by the other. After further meetings with each team, the mediator develops a proposed settlement for presentation to both parties that will end the impasse.

The fact-finding process leads to a set of independently developed recommendations for a settlement of the impasse. Prior to fact finding, the parties prepare their cases with supporting documentation and arguments. The fact-finder considers the cases and develops a report. The fact-finder's report may be accepted or rejected by one or both parties. If the report is made public, it may be persuasive in the parties' eventual acceptance.

If neither mediation nor fact finding is effective in resolving an impasse, binding arbitration is often the result. The arbitration can be voluntary or mandatory, advisory or binding. However, if mediation and/or fact finding has not been successful, binding arbitration is the only viable solution short of a strike.

In arbitration, the parties usually have the right to select or reject names from a list of potential arbitrators. The selected arbitrator conducts a hearing at which each party presents its written exhibits and oral testimony. Within a reasonable period after the hearing, the arbitrator's decision is issued. If binding arbitration is used, the decision resolves the impasse and the arbitrator's report becomes the "settlement."

CONTRACT ADMINISTRATION

A successful collective bargaining process leads to an agreement or contract that determines the conditions of employment for its duration. If an educational administrator is to be an effective and respected leader in the school community, it is essential that he or she "knows the contract." Failing to do so will lead to embarrassing contract breeches that will undermine the administrator's competence and any culture of trust that has been established. Thus, principals and other administrators should participate in training sessions about the newly adopted contract. Preparation of an administrator's manual, which includes interpretation of contract clauses, procedures for processing grievances, and contractual deadlines, should take place.

SUMMARY

Power might be one of the least understood, but most important areas of educational administration. This chapter described the sources and uses of power in institutions. Position power, personal power, and resource- and information-based power were all described herein.

Continued focus was also given to looking at negotiation as the ritualized use of power in organizations. Two bargaining paradigms, distributive and integrative, were described and compared. Then, the process of negotiation was outlined; the steps include preparation, model selection and strategy development, negotiating an agreement, and contract administration.

It is likely that most educational administrators will not be integrally involved in the bargaining process because that duty is usually assigned to a collective bargaining specialist. However, all educational administrators will be responsible for the administration of the contract and ultimately be involved in contract grievances.

It is important to know the process whereby the contract was established and to know the nuances of its implementation. Many an administrator has been rendered ineffective, and has even been considered incompetent because of an insufficient knowledge of the details and implications of the labor agreement. Thus, a thorough understanding of the document and a humane implementation of it are essential elements to an educational administrator's eventual success.

IMPLICATIONS FOR PRACTICE: EMPOWERMENT FOR SUCCESS CASE STUDY

Charlotte Graham is the new principal of Springhill High School and it is her first day on the job. As she reviews her daily schedule, she is reminded of the upcoming meeting that will take place immediately following the lunch hour. Charlotte will meet for the first time Marie Wilson, the teacher union representative. Ms. Wilson's reputation as a direct, very assertive (borderline aggressive) administrator precedes her. Charlotte has already been forewarned of this impending encounter and has been given advice to present as a strong-willed individual who reached her respective position by aggressively pursuing professional goals. There's an air about the office that reeks of an intent to show dominance.

The scenario here is not unlike many that occur at educational institutions of all levels. This situation reflects the exercise of power in an organization. What types of power might one expect to observe during this encounter at Springhill High School? Recognizing, using, and dealing with power differences is implicit in negotiation, which is a process for reconciling different, often incompatible, interests of interdependent parties. At Springhill High School, both Charlotte Graham and Marie Wilson have power. How well each one uses her power and negotiation skills will determine her effectiveness.

DIAGNOSTIC DEBRIEF

Here are some questions that may be helpful in assessing the distribution of power in an institution:

- Is power appropriately shared?
- What type of negotiations occurs in the school district or higher education institution and do these negotiations tend to be distributive or integrative?
- What degree of preparation takes place to ensure contract language is understood by all?
- Are provisions made for the proper administration of the contract?

Chapter 9

Comprehensive and Strategic Planning Models

Planning is all, but plans are nothing.

—Dwight D. Eisenhower

Blanchard and Johnson posit that the effective manager must spend time developing goals and placing them in the context of a vision. There is much to be said as to the wisdom of this assertion, especially in educational settings. There is a plethora of scholarly school research that corroborates their recommendation. A number of studies have found that when schools develop clear and agreed-upon goals that are duly promulgated, they are usually effective. Thus, effective educational administrators need to develop an educational vision that is mutually acceptable and is understood by all components of the school community.

In some circles exactly what constitutes an educational vision seems to be shrouded in mystery. Actually, the process of developing an educational vision is not all that complex. The first step is to identify a list of broad goals. This step in the process should be done in conjunction with representatives from all components of the school community. Otherwise, there will be no sense of "ownership" on the part of the school community which will jeopardize the successful implementation of the vision and its goals. "All Children Achieving" is an example of such a broad goal.

The next step in the process is to merge and prioritize the goals, and summarize them in the form of a short and concise statement. The following is an example of a vision statement:

Our vision for the Exeter School System is that all of our graduating students, regardless of ability, will say that "I have received an excellent education that has prepared me to be an informed citizen and leader in my community." In addition, our students will be committed to a process of lifelong learning and the making of a better world by living the ideals of fairness and justice and service to others.

The key concepts in the foregoing vision statement are "all students can learn," "academic excellence," "leadership," "lifelong learning," "values," and community "service." It is these concepts or goals that the ten-minute educational leader needs to stress in all forms of communication and in all of his or her interpersonal relations with the various members of the school community.

The final step in the process is the "institutionalizing" of the vision. This step ensures that the vision endures even when the leadership in the institution changes. Operationalizing and placing the important concepts of the vision into the official policies and procedures of the school system is one important way of helping to institutionalize the educational vision and incorporate it into the school culture.

Another way of institutionalizing a vision is by encouraging the development of "heroes" who embody the institution's vision and "tribal storytellers," who promulgate it (Palestini, 2012). It has been often heard that individuals in various organizations describe a colleague as "an institution around here." Heroes such as these do more to establish the organizational culture of an institution than any manual or policies and procedures handbook ever could. The senior faculty member who is recognized and respected for their knowledge of the subject matter as well as their humane treatment of students is an invaluable asset to an educational institution. They are a symbol of what the institution stands for—what it represents.

It is the presence of heroes that sustains the reputation of the institution and allows the workforce to feel good about itself and about where it works. The deeds and accomplishments of these heroes need to be promulgated and need to become part of the folklore of the institution.

The deeds of these heroes are usually perpetuated by the "tribal storytellers" in an organization. These are the individuals who know the history of the organization and relate it through stories of its former and present heroes. An effective leader encourages the tribal storytellers, knowing that they are serving an invaluable service in an institution. They work at the process of institutional renewal. They allow the institution to continuously improve. They preserve and revitalize the values of the institution. They mitigate the tendency of institutions, especially educational institutions, to become bureaucratic. Every institution has heroes and storytellers. It is the educational leader's job to see to it that things like manuals and handbooks don't replace them.

A STRATEGIC PLANNING PROCESS FOR EDUCATIONAL INSTITUTIONS

Ten specifically identified activities would be included in a strategic plan for academic planning in educational institutions. They include the following:

1. Develop a mission statement. The process of developing a mission statement involves establishing a strong group consensus about the unique purposes of the educational institution and its place in the community that it serves. The process of development of the mission will set the tone for all further planning activity. Most often, educational institutions have an existing mission. However, the planning process should not begin until there is broad acceptance of the current mission. Many times, the mission needs to be revised to adapt to current circumstances before the process can continue.

The educational vision of the school is derived from the mission statement. It is often a concise summary of the mission or how one expects mission to play out for the future.

2. Develop a set of institutional goals. The institution should next develop a set of goals that it deems appropriate in the accomplishment of its mission. Goals are more specific and give direction to the action that needs to take place to achieve them. The goals should be expressed in terms that would promote easy assessment. It should be clear to an objective observer whether they have been achieved. An example of a goal that would be derived from the mission statement listed earlier would be, "to provide an education that addresses all dimensions of a student's character, mental, psychological, physical, and spiritual."

3. Develop learning outcomes statements. The process of developing student learning outcomes statements, including transitional outcomes, should include the outcomes students must achieve in order to meet the institutional goals and progress from one level to the next. For example, from the primary to the intermediate level, intermediate level to middle level, and middle level to the high school program. An example of a typical outcome statement might be, "upon completing the American history course, the student will have the ability to research a topic in history, analyze its causes and effects and determine its implications for the future."

Ways of authentically assessing these educational outcomes also need to be developed. The current emphasis on outcomes-based education (OBE), authentic assessment, and portfolio assessment focuses quite heavily on this step in the planning process.

4. Establish stakeholder groups. Following the previous step, in which developed outcome statements were drafted, a group of internal and external stakeholder groups are solicited to provide important, critical feedback. This step helps ensure collection of unique and distinct perspectives from

a variety of constituency groups. Accepting a wide range of perspectives provides for more robust sharing and understanding of the outcomes as they relate to different interests. Transparency of the planning process, goals, and outcomes is provided as a result of internal and external stakeholder involvement. Lastly, this step provides outreach for extended community engagement from neighbors, local business owners, parents, civic and municipal leaders, and so on.

5. Develop the curriculum. The essence of the conversion from a class time-based system to a student learning outcomes-based system is the revision of all academic courses to reflect student learning outcome statements. The courses should be developed to include a number of the learning outcomes determined earlier. Courses should be developed until all of the learning outcomes have been incorporated into at least one of the courses.

6. Conduct a comprehensive needs analysis. The needs analysis is a crucial part of the strategic planning process. It must involve a comprehensive identification of both internal and external strengths and weaknesses and include an analysis of instructional practices. The process should rely on both quantitative and qualitative data.

A needs analysis should involve all "stakeholder" groups within the local community, giving each an opportunity to provide both hard data and informed opinion. Methods for data gathering for a comprehensive need analysis may include any and/or all of the following: gap analysis, landscape scanning, competitor benchmarking, and a formal SWOT (strengths, weaknesses, opportunities, and threats) analysis. The result of the needs analysis should be the main tool in developing priority goal areas for action planning.

7. Develop a list of priorities. Priorities are identified by a process that applies the information accumulated during the needs analysis to the list of general institutional goals identified earlier. Those goals that show need for developmental action are prioritized on the basis of their relationship to the identified mission and on the severity of the need. One or more action plans or strategies are developed for each of the priorities.

8. Develop specific action plans. One or more action plans or strategies are to be developed for each of the priority goal areas. The action plans are to identify specific actions to be taken to meet the identified priority needs. Action plans should include

 a. Objectives
 b. Major strategies to be completed
 c. Projected time lines or completion dates
 d. The person or group responsible
 e. Estimated costs, if any
 f. Evaluation or assessment questions

9. Develop an assessment plan. The assessment plan ascertains the degree to which the student learning outcomes are achieved. The assessment plan should include the following:

a. The general purpose of the assessments
b. A description of the process to be used to develop and analyze portfolios of student work, including a variety of strategies
c. A description of assessment procedures to be used
d. A description of how the assessment results will be used
e. A description of how the school will assist students who have not demonstrated mastery of the outcomes
f. A description of the process for notifying the public of assessment results

10. Prepare a professional development plan. The final step in the academic planning process is to prepare a professional development plan to train and prepare the staff to implement the plans. This step is especially important if new and innovative approaches are required to implement the strategic plan.

STRATEGIC PLANNING MODELS

The previous ten-step process provides a fairly common approach used in K–12 environments. However, there are other models that some organizations may choose to follow. The following sections provide context for two specific models, Bryson's (2011) A, B, Cs of strategic planning and Sanaghan's (2009) collaborative strategic planning process.

A, B, Cs of Strategic Planning

Planning for the future is a vital function for organizations. A popularly method used for gathering data, analyzing possibilities and challenges, and determining a pathway for success is the development of a strategic plan (or often called *comprehensive* plan in K–12 settings). Bryson (2011) defines strategic planning as "a deliberative, disciplined effort to produce fundamental decision and actions that shape and guide what an organization (or other entity) is, what it does, and why it does it." This definition informs the three-step process outlined in his model.

Bryson offers a three-part model for organizations to follow when creating a strategic plan. The three components are (1) vision, mission, and goals, (2) strategy formulation, and (3) strategy implementation.

A, B, Cs of strategic planning is a model that employs a targeted question and tools to guide organizations from one component of the model to another.

For example, asking "where you are" and "where you want to be" leads to vision, mission, and goal development. Strategy formulation takes place in the space between "where you are" and "how to get there." Finally, strategy implementation is created when organizations explore "how to get there" and "where you want to be."

Gathering stakeholders to vet answers to the three principle questions lays the foundation for goal development. After goals are determined, organizational leaders meet to develop objectives, or action statements, that support work toward goal accomplishment. Finally, goal metrics and resources needed for plan implementation are determined.

To offer an example, a strategic planning goal might be *enriching academic quality and distinction*. This goal would then be supported by several objectives such as *to develop and support new teaching spaces and cutting-edge facilities* and *to implement a new inclusive instructional model*. Measurable metrics for the goal's objectives must then be created. In the aforementioned example, a metric for the first objective might be the creation of a campus master plan that will be used to address facility renovation needs. Resources needed for this metric would include allocated funds to hire an architectural firm to assist with the creation of a master plan. A finished comprehensive plan commonly has four to six major goals with two to four objectives under each goal.

Collaborative Strategic Planning

Different from the A, B, Cs model of strategic planning, Sanaghan (2009) provides a unique framework for consideration. This model seeks high engagement and inclusion from multiple stakeholders in order for the planning process to be efficient and effective in its execution.

A key component of Sanaghan's process is the creation of a highly credible internal planning task force (PTF), given the responsibility for steering the organization through the entire collaborative process. Acting as a change agent, the PTF "taps into and builds the capacity of the institution to think and plan in collaborative and inclusive ways" (Sanaghan, 2009). Throughout the entire planning process, stakeholders are given a voice and remain active in plan development activities.

Aside from the collaborative nature of this model, an additional value that must be maintained is transparency. Opportunities for sharing and seeking feedback are maintained throughout plan development as a way of enhancing stakeholder buy-in and ensuring plan transparency. In the end, this framework grants maximum stakeholder involvement and contribution, allowing for the creation of a robust future trajectory for the organization.

As its name suggests, this model gives great intentionality to collaboration. The overall framework is outlined in a five-phase linear process. The phases are as follows: (1) getting organized, (2) data gathering, (3) sensemaking, (4) vision conference, and (5) goals conference.

- Within the first phase, organizational leadership widely communicates the purpose of the strategic planning process to garner enthusiasm for stakeholder interest. This is also the phase in which the PTF is established. In this phase the organizational leader also confirms their role as a planning process champion, but not driver or controller of the development of the plan; these roles are reserved for the PTF.
- The *data gathering and engagement* phase in this model is considered one of the most crucial. Within this phase, the PTF engages in meaningful discussions and dialogue with as many different and diverse stakeholder groups as possible. The PTF is also provided training to teach them several activities designed to ensure lots of cross-sectional involvement and engagement. Data gathering work is completed through face-to-face engagement, interviews, focus groups, and survey data-collection techniques.
- In the *sensemaking* phase, the PTF meets to review all data that was collected in phase two. Sifting through this mountain of data, they conclude their deliberations with a series of authored concept papers. These papers offer a brief and concise description of major themes determined as a result of analyzing all available and relevant data. Once written and reviewed by others in the PTF, the concept papers are then made public and are circulated to all members of the organization.
- A one-day, highly interactive meeting is held, called the *visions conference*. This workshop brings together between fifty and seventy-five stakeholders from both internal and external groups. There are three functions that take place at the visions conference. First, participants review and discuss the concept papers written by the PTF. Next, stakeholders are divided into smaller groups and asked to discuss and share from their unique perspective important ideas for the future direction of the organization. Creating a *preferred future* is the last task of the visions conference. Still working in smaller groups, stakeholders are asked to frame their future vision for the organization into a five-year framework. They then give formal presentations to the entire conference audience. Facilitated discussions after the presentations help identify common ground themes that are then written into a drafted vision statement for the organization. This is then shared and distributed to all stakeholders within the organization.
- The last phase of the collaborative strategic planning process is the *goals conference*. The PTF convenes for a one- to two-day working meeting to create a broad plan for implementation. The vision statement and concept papers are referenced to establish goals and strategic themes. Action plans are then drafted for each identified goal. Following the goals conference,

the action plans are sent to organizational leaders for discussion and review. Once approved, the plan is published in its final copy and distributed widely. In many cases, leaders who will oversee implementation of different goals have been identified from their participation in the visions conference or previous planning engagement activities.

SUMMARY

A strategic plan is a guide grounded in mission to identify core values that informs vision and alignment toward established immediate and long-term objectives. It defines measurable priorities, action plans, for internal/external stakeholders that demonstrate a commitment to organizational growth, and momentum toward future goals.

This chapter outlines common steps employed by organizations when developing a comprehensive plan. Additionally, two specific frameworks are shared with the readership. Both Bryson's (2011) A, B, Cs strategic planning process and Sanaghan's (2009) collaborative strategic planning process provide differentiated methodologies for consideration in the development of an organization's future plan.

IMPLICATIONS FOR PRACTICE: COMPREHENSIVE AND STRATEGIC PLANNING MODELS CASE STUDY

Rylan Cannon Middle School (RCMS) is a typical suburban secondary school located in a medium-sized city in the mid-west. It plays host to 643 sixth, seventh, and eighth graders. The district is sufficiently resourced by property taxes and parent involvement is adequate (not excellent, but not scant either).

Eight years ago, RCMS created its first ten-year comprehensive plan, which has brought about positive change. Notably, students and teachers now benefit from a school mission statement and vision, an improved curriculum, greater focus on teacher professional development, and renovated facilities.

As Jamie Williams enters her seventh year as an assistant principal at RCMS, she is reminded that the current ten-year comprehensive plan only has two years left until its completion. As such, the principal has approached Williams to lead a steering committee for a new strategic plan that will guide the success of RCMS over the next seven to ten years. Despite Jamie's experience and likeability as a school administrator, she has much apprehension about this new daunting task, having never served on a strategic planning taskforce.

Later that night, in the privacy of her home, she begins a google search for strategic plan "how to" resources. Initially, this only exacerbates her anxiety regarding this task. After two hours of trolling the internet she finally stumbles upon one strategic planning model that looks promising. She is immediately attracted to this model because it provides clear structure for shared input from school stakeholders. Jamie places an order for several books on this model and waits their arrival with much anticipation. As a type-A personality, Jamie looks forward to outlining a process that will ensure an effective planning process that will take place.

DIAGNOSTIC DEBRIEF

Here are a few questions that can assess an institution's understanding and commitment to its goals:

- Does a mission statement exist? Does it accurately reflect the current aspirations of the organization?
- Does a vision statement exist? Does it need to be amended?
- Does a strategic plan exist? If yes, what goals have been achieved and which ones remain?
- Are the goals, objectives, and strategies clear and measurable?
- Are they known and understood by the school community?
- Is the planning process ongoing?

Chapter 10

Leadership through Change

Change will not come if we wait for some other person or if we wait for some other time. We are the ones we've been waiting for. We are the change that we seek.

—*President Barack Obama*

Changing an educational institution or system has been described as a near impossible and laborious task, much like requesting a cruise liner to make a U-turn in gale force winds on the open ocean. In some cases, resistance to change is so extreme that even the scenario described in the cruise ship metaphor is an understatement. Despite its difficulty, the process of change is absolutely necessary if an organization is to continually improve. Thus, to be an effective leader, especially in the transformational style, an administrator must become a change agent and master the process that can bring change about effectively.

AN INTEGRATED APPROACH TO CHANGE

The literature is replete with various suggested change processes. Many of them contain elements that are helpful in leading to successful transformation, but few contain all of the necessary elements. As a result, through the process of trial and error, the following recommendations have been developed regarding the process for change. It is called an integrated change process because although there are distinct steps in the process, the key to their successful implementation is that many of them are implemented simultaneously rather than sequentially.

In an earlier work, entitled *Ten Steps to Educational Reform: Making Change Happen,* the following steps in the process were suggested (Palestini, 2004):

- Establishing a climate for change
- Assessing the need for change
- Creating a sense of urgency
- Assessing favorable and opposing forces
- Selecting among alternatives
- Promoting ownership
- Providing professional development
- Operationalizing the change
- Evaluating the change
- Institutionalizing the change

Most attempts at effecting change in the form of educational reform fail because leaders have no formal plan at all or do not engage in all the steps in the process. Other failures occur when administrators try to implement the reform by following the change process steps sequentially rather than simultaneously and get bogged down in one or another of the steps, unable to bring the process to closure.

Whether it be an apparently insignificant change, such as deciding between the homogenous or the heterogeneous grouping of students (tracking), or what form of assessment should be used in course selection, or a more significant reform, such as whether tuition vouchers should be used to restructure and reform public education, it is suggested that the implementation of these steps in an integrated way will successfully bring about the desired change.

ESTABLISHING A CLIMATE FOR CHANGE

E. Mark Hanson, in his text entitled *Educational Administration and Organizational Behavior,* describes an incident regarding the process of change. Always interested in the processes of school improvement, he once asked the superintendent of a large, urban school district, "How does change come about around here?" She thought for a moment. "Well," she replied, "there is the normal way and the miraculous way. The normal way," she continued, "is where the heavens part and the angels come down and do the change for us. The miraculous way is when we do it ourselves" (Hanson, 1991).

If one has established a climate of change at his or her institution, change will come to be expected. It will be perceived as something positive and routine. The need for change in the context of continuous improvement should be articulated constantly by institutional leaders.

College presidents, superintendents, and principals should set the tone for change by taking every opportunity to articulate its necessity and model it in their own leadership. For example, the faculty convocations can be occasions for articulating the notion that if the institution is to progress, academically and operationally, it must be open to change. At the initial meeting, the possible changes that are anticipated during the upcoming academic year can be shared. At subsequent faculty meetings, the need for change can be reinforced.

In addition to articulating the need for change, to promote a positive school climate the leader must model a tolerance for change. Even if something as simple as changing the color of the school lockers every two or three years or changing the format of faculty meetings to incorporate innovative concepts like cooperative learning and shared decision-making, the leader needs to lead by example. The leader must be perceived as being open to new ideas and providing a climate in which creativity is fostered. In other words, leaders must "be the change that they expect in others."

If a positive climate for change is to be established, another requisite is an environment of trust and respect. Institutions do not amount to anything without the people who make them what they are. The individuals most influential in making institutions what they are, are essentially volunteers. The very best teachers and administrators can work anywhere they please. So, in a sense, they volunteer to work where they do. Educational leaders would do far better if they looked on and treated salaried employees with the deference with which they treat volunteers.

ASSESSING A NEED

The next step in the integrated change process is the needs assessment. Unfortunately, this step is often ignored. Many educational leaders become enamored with one educational reform or another and try to implement it whether or not there is an identified and agreed-upon need. Reforms, such as the whole-language approach to reading, cooperative learning, block scheduling, interdisciplinary curricula, distance learning, and even site-based management, have been adopted arbitrarily by misguided educational administrators. When implemented without a needs assessment these changes are almost always destined to failure.

Ordinarily, a needs assessment calls for a review of existing data and may require some surveying of the various components or stakeholders of the school community. There is always a certain risk in a needs assessment. In the process of uncovering needs, one might also raise expectations that all of the respondent's concerns will be addressed.

Fundamental to effecting change is priority setting and focus; thus, not all needs can be met immediately. Resources are in short supply, and difficult, sometimes painful decisions have to be made about which from an array of crucial needs requires attention. Three reference groups are especially important to the needs assessment and the change process: students and parents, professional staff, and educational policymakers. Oftentimes, it is the students and/or parents who are left out of the process. Leaving them out, of course, has distribution of power and motivation implications and empirical research suggests that inclusion is much preferred to exclusion.

Data about students are readily available in the records a typical educational institution generates and maintains. Standardized test scores, attendance records, free or reduced-price lunch recipients, percentage of students with disabilities, transportation reports, and a host of other official and unofficial data serve as sources for developing a profile of the students in the school or school district. Informal discussions with colleagues, other professionals, and the students and parents themselves are another source of information. Student focus groups and systematic observation by both teachers and administrators are still other ways of assessing whether there is a need for change in the school.

Central office personnel, local and state board members, state departments of educational, legislators, the United States Department of Education, and education advocacy groups should also be consulted to identify the needs of the educational institution. Lastly, the reports of accrediting agencies, such as the Middle States Association, Phi Beta Kappa, and the American Association of Colleges and Schools of Business (AACSB) can be valuable tools for assessing the needs of an institution.

CREATING A SENSE OF URGENCY

Because a natural instinct is to resist change, to effect a needed change, a sense of alarm or urgency oftentimes must be created to effect change. To overcome the innate sense of inertia, the dire consequences of remaining in the status quo need to be articulated by the change agent.

There are a number of ways to create a sense of urgency, including citing comparable data from similar institutions and projected student enrollment declines. But in creating a sense of urgency, the change agent must be aware that individuals and groups are often moved by dissimilar forces. In other words, what might cause a sense of urgency in one person might cause a sense of hopelessness in another, which in turn can lead to a self-fulfilling prophesy.

Thus, creating a sense of urgency or stress can have both functional and dysfunctional outcomes. Whether stress takes a constructive or destructive course is influenced by the sociocultural context in which the stress occurs. A culture of trust and respect is a considerable asset.

Effective educational administrators learn how to create functional conflict and manage dysfunctional conflict. They develop and practice techniques for diagnosing the causes and nature of stress and transform it into a productive force that fosters needed change in the institution.

ASSESSING FAVORABLE AND OPPOSING FORCES

Accurate assessment of the forces that affect proposed reform is perhaps the most important step in the integrated change process. Correctly identifying the forces that favor the reform and those that oppose it is crucial to effective implementation of the change. Further, the interventions chosen to neutralize the forces against change and enhance the forces in favor of it are instrumental to its eventual success.

The forces resistant to change can be considerable. These forces range from simple ignorance of an individual to the complex vested interests that exist. As the comic strip character Pogo phrased it, "We have met the enemy and he is us."

The forces resistant to change are an important part of the organization's environment or culture. They must be diagnosed, understood, and considered in the targeting process and in selecting a change strategy. According to Richard Carlson, a major organizational feature that contributes to resistance to change is the domestication of public schools and other educational institutions. A domesticated organization has many properties of the monopoly: it does not have to compete for resources, except in a very limited area; it has a steady flow of clients; and its survival is guaranteed.

Although private schools and colleges do not possess all the same domesticating characteristics in the way that public schools do, many of the teachers view their institutions in this way. One often hears the college professor or the private school teacher proclaim in the light of declining enrollments, "That's the administration's problem" (Carlson, 1990).

FORCE-FIELD ANALYSIS

To understand the shifting forces that affect a change, leaders can use an analytical technique called force-field analysis, which views a problem as a product of forces working in different, often opposite directions. An organization, or any of its subsystems, maintains the status quo when the sum of opposing forces is zero. When forces in one direction exceed forces in the opposite one, the organization or subsystem moves in the direction of the greater forces. For example, if forces for change exceed forces against change, then change is likely to occur (Lewin, 1951).

To move the educational institution toward a different desired state requires increasing the forces for change in that direction, decreasing the forces against change in that direction, or both. Generally, reducing resistance forces creates less tension in the system and fewer unanticipated consequences than increasing forces for change. Suppose an institution was moving from homogenous to heterogeneous grouping. Reducing the resistances to the changes created by the introduction of heterogeneous grouping increases the likelihood of the changeover. When the administrators and staff no longer resist change, the present state moves closer to the desired state.

Consider again examples of heterogeneous grouping. Moving from homogenous grouping in the form of tracking to the more egalitarian heterogeneous grouping is bound to encounter resistance. What are the opposing forces that one can anticipate? Certainly, some of the teaching staff will be against the change because it will entail more small-group instruction and adapting their lesson plans to a variety of ability levels.

On the contrary, what are the forces in favor of change? Once again, one can anticipate that certain of the faculty will favor the more inclusive approach that is embodied in heterogeneous grouping. A savvy administrator will be able to apply interventions that would neutralize the opposition and mobilize the forces in favor of this change. Using force-field analysis in a systematic way can be very helpful in bringing about desired change (see figure 10.1).

DEVELOPING AND SELECTING ALTERNATIVES

While the already-mentioned steps in the integrated change process are being addressed, the change agent should establish a committee or task force of "believers" to begin developing alternatives that would address the perceived need(s). Ideally, a deliberative consideration of the various alternatives should be undertaken, and the ones that best satisfy the cost/benefits analysis should be chosen. All too often, however, "the powers that be" have arbitrarily chosen the preferred alternative and the change agent is expected simply to implement it. This would be an example of what a wise leader never wants to do, namely, "back him or herself into a corner."

Another phenomenon that sometimes occurs during this phase of the change process is the tendency to satisfice, or choose the alternative that

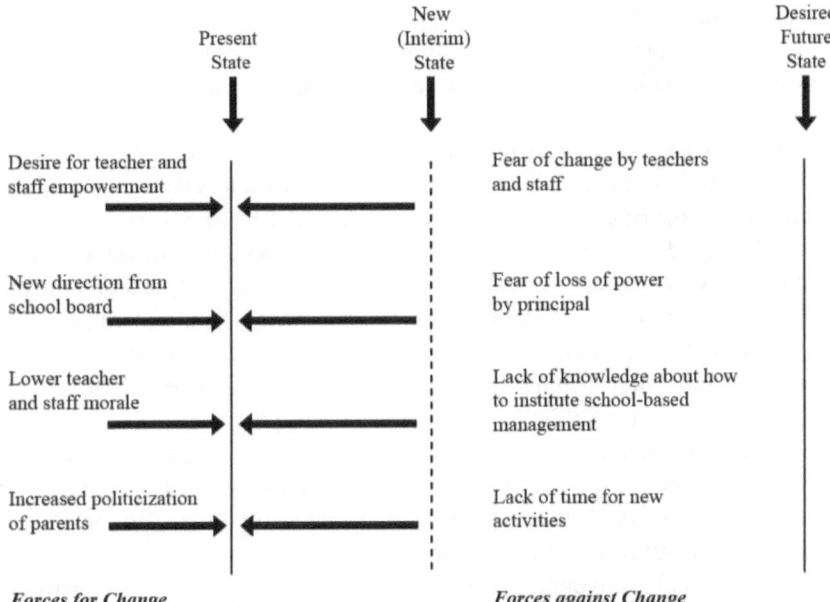

Figure 10.1 Force-Field Analysis.

offends the fewest individuals and/or groups, rather than choosing the best alternative. "Satisficing" is a term coined by Herbert Simon, a Nobel Prize winner in economics, who was critical of the so-called rational model of decision-making, which indicates that decision makers develop and analyze all of the possible alternatives and select the best one available (Simon, 1960).

According to Simon, at a certain point in the decision-making process, rather than the best-possible alternative being chosen, in the interest of efficiency the decision maker will satisfice, or sacrifice the optimal for a solution or alternative that is satisfactory or good enough. For example, if a school is trying to decide between the traditional phonics-approach versus the whole-language approach to teaching reading, the change agent(s) may satisfice and choose an integrated model that combines what it believes to be the best aspects of both the phonics and whole-language approaches. Thus, the change agent may sacrifice the optimal solution for one that satisfies the greatest number of constituencies.

PROMOTING A SENSE OF OWNERSHIP

It is a truism in education that if a change or reform is to be implemented successfully, it must have the support and acceptance of the faculty and staff. Consequently, it is often heard managers suggest that a new program does not have a chance of succeeding unless the employees take ownership of it. This assertion is agreeable to most. But how does a leader effectively promote employee ownership? The following four steps are suggested:

- Respect people. As was earlier indicated, this starts with appreciating the diverse gifts that individuals bring to the organization. The key is to dwell on the strengths of coworkers, rather than on their weaknesses.
- Let belief guide policy and practice. Developing a culture of civility in an institution was previously mentioned as an important aspect of a strong learning environment. If there is an environment of mutual respect and trust, the institution will flourish. Leaders need to let their belief or value systems guide their behavior. Style is merely a consequence of what is believed and what is in the hearts of those occupying the space.
- Recognize the need for covenants. Contractual agreements cover such things as salary, fringe benefits, and working conditions. They are part of organization life, and there is a legitimate need for them. But in today's educational institutions, where the best people working in schools are similar to volunteers, covenantal relationships are needed. The best workers might choose their employers. They usually choose the institution where they work based on reasons less tangible than salaries and fringe benefits. Covenantal relationships enable educational institutions to be civil, hospitable, and are understanding of individuals' differences and unique natures.
- Understand that culture counts more than structure. An educational institution recently went through a particularly traumatic time when the credibility of the administration was questioned by the faculty and staff. Various organizational development consultants were interviewed to facilitate a healing process. Most of the consultants spoke of making the necessary structural changes to create a culture of trust. The consultant who was hired, however, began with the attitude that organizational structure has nothing to do with building trust. Interpersonal relations based on mutual respect and an atmosphere of goodwill is what creates a culture of trust.

PROVIDING STAFF DEVELOPMENT

Very often, staff development, an essential part of the change process, is neglected or overlooked completely. Many educational reforms have failed because of an enthusiastic but ill-advised leader who has tried to implement a change before engaging in staff development. Sometimes, even when staff development is provided, it is poor staff development. Negative responses to staff development are often the result of a history of poor experiences with activities such as in-service training.

The most important resource in an institution is its staff. When the staff's thinking is congruent with organizational needs, and when the staff is well-trained, adaptive, and motivated, effective schools result. To achieve this goal requires attention to the various ways in which human potential can be realized and to the variety of needs that any particular person and group might have at any particular stage of development. Providing adequate and effective staff development enables individuals to reach their potential; it enables them to succeed.

OPERATIONALIZING CHANGE

At this point in the integrated change process, operationalization of the change takes place, or gives form to a vision. Although careful preparation for change increases the chances of success, it does not guarantee effective action. Placing the plan in operation requires the establishment of the organizational structure that will best suit the change, and development of an assessment process to determine if the change is remaining on course. Briefing sessions, special seminars, or other means of information dissemination must permeate the change effort. Operationalizing the change must include procedures for keeping all participants informed about the change activities and its effects.

EVALUATING CHANGE

The next step in the integrated change process is the evaluation of the change. Authentic assessment is a topical issue in education these days. Many are questioning exactly how to assess performance most accurately, effectively, and fairly. After generations of focusing on program inputs, stressing program *outcomes* as an authentic measure of a program's effectiveness is gaining in popularity. An emphasis on outcomes versus inputs is much preferred in assessing the true effectiveness of a change or reform.

The change agent(s) should collect data about the nature and effectiveness of the change. The results of the evaluation indicate whether the change process is complete, or a return to an earlier stage should occur. The criteria for success should be specified in advance of a change effort. These criteria can be culturally linked and varied; they also should be closely related to the *goals* of the reform. If ineffective outcomes result from the introduction of a whole-language-based reading program, for example, the process should return to an earlier stage, such as needs assessment, to determine if the institution is really in need of it, and if the school community has been properly prepared.

INSTITUTIONALIZING CHANGE

Provided that the evaluation process shows that the reform has been effective, the change then should become institutionalized; that is, the changed processes and/or programs should be established as permanent ways of operating. Otherwise, when the current change agent(s) leaves, the change may not be perpetuated.

In ideal circumstances, reform should become part of the organizational culture. It is in this way that a legacy is created from which future generations of students, parents, faculty, and staff can benefit. The results of a failure to institutionalize a reform are often seen at the state and federal Department of Education levels. How many times has a governor or president set an effective educational agenda, only to have it scuttled and replaced with a different agenda by the subsequent administration? If a successful change is to prevail over time, it must be institutionalized.

Educational leaders, therefore, must build learning communities, ones that emphasize ongoing adaptability and self-generation, thereby emphasizing coping and looking at the world creatively. Peter Senge says, "Leaders in learning organizations are responsible for building organizations where people are continually expanding their capabilities to shape their future—that is, leaders are responsible for learning." Where better to implement Senge's ideas regarding a learning community than in an educational institution (Senge, 1990)?

CONCLUSION

Edwards Deming said that healthy organizations are ones that are continually improving. Continuous improvement assumes change. Therefore, if an educational leader is to be effective, he or she must become an agent of change (Demings, 2000).

Mastering the change process requires a leader to know and understand the steps involved in planning a successful transformation in an organization. If the change can take place in an atmosphere of mutual trust and respect, its chances for success are maximized.

The suggested model for effecting change is to access the organization to ascertain the need for change, to diagnose the forces that influence change, and to implement the change by maximizing the forces in favor of the change and minimizing the forces opposing the change.

Once the change is made, a thorough evaluation of its effectiveness precedes the final step of institutionalizing the change, which ensures its continuation—even after the change agent is no longer present.

A key step in the process is the diagnosing of the forces influencing change. A useful technique in assessing these factors is called force-field analysis. This technique allows one to determine the forces in favor and those opposed to change and to plan interventions that would mobilize the forces in favor of change and mitigate the forces opposing change. If one can effectively orchestrate this step of the process, the desired change will most likely occur. In many ways, successfully affecting a transformational change necessitates the collective use of all of an administrator's knowledge and skills. It can be seen as the culminating activity of an educational leader.

IMPLICATIONS FOR PRACTICE: LEADERSHIP THROUGH CHANGE CASE STUDY

Market View High School, a comprehensive high school with a faculty of 210 and a diverse student body of over 3,000 students, is headed by an administrative staff composed of a principal and two vice principals.

In the past, Market View was a part of a region known as District Five. Communication would filter from the superintendent to the deputy superintendent for school operations, to the associate superintendent for curriculum, to the district superintendents, who would then filter information to the principals. The principals would then disseminate information to department heads and school staff. This communication structure represents the classical chain of command. Communication was transmitted from the central office through clearly defined channels, and each employee understood the sanctity of the chain of command.

Three years ago, when Matthew Goldstein was recruited as superintendent of schools, he mapped out a broad plan for change that affected the traditional hierarchical structure. The districts became clusters, and the district superintendents became cluster leaders. Each cluster provides leadership and support for reform in small school groupings covering K–12. Each high school and its feeder schools form a cluster. The centralized bureaucracy shrank, and clusters were given greater authority to support efforts of schools to plan improvements. The cluster office for the Market View Cluster is now located in the basement of Market View High School. This set the stage for ongoing conflict between the principal, Jack Stern, and the cluster leader, Rita Moyer.

For the past four years, Jack has been the principal of Market View High School, after a 25-year stint at a sister high school in the same city. He was a former gym teacher who worked his way up from physical education department chair to vice principal and then to principal. He thrives working in very traditional settings where reforms, such as small learning communities, professional learning communities, or teachers conducting classroom research, are uncommon. He entered Market View totally unprepared for the level of activism evident in his faculty.

Jack also adopted a laissez-faire style of supervision and left the day-to-day running of the curricular program to department heads and small learning community coordinators. He held weekly meetings with the school leadership teams and insisted that all ideas about curricular change or school activities be submitted to him for formal approval prior to a discussion with the general faculty. The school does not have a home and school association, nor does it have a pupil support committee. Both of these structures are necessary features of school communities under Superintendent Goldstein's "Children Achieving" agenda.

Rita, a former principal of an elementary school in the cluster, became cluster leader for Market View two years ago. She entered with definite ideas for the reform of teaching and learning at the high school. She had heard of Mr. Stern's laissez-faire leadership style, and she was determined to provide a different kind of leadership.

Rita initially adopted a human relations approach and presented herself as a collegial leader. She held meetings with school administrators, department heads, small learning community leaders, the custodians, and non-tenured classroom assistants. She called numerous meetings and engaged teachers and other staff members in professional development opportunities that often took teachers out of the classroom, often for two or more days. Rita often failed to notify the principal of meetings she scheduled with "his" staff, and a few times he was stuck with trying to secure substitute coverage for teachers away on "school business" without his knowledge. When it came to the principal, Rita traded collegiality for autocracy. She became quite autocratic in her directives to the principal. She chastised him for not having a home and school association and for not having a pupil support committee.

Rita's political savvy brought the cluster and Goldstein's "Children Achieving" program millions of dollars. She brought together a grant-writing team that secured the Market View Cluster's IBM Reinventing Education Grant. This brought $2 million of equipment and technical support to the cluster.

Teachers from multiple schools within the cluster program received much needed integrated classroom technology to assist with differentiated instruction as a result of the additional financial support. Several of the participating teachers who held other leadership roles at Market View were often scheduled for cluster meetings at the same time the principal scheduled mandatory professional development activities. This often resulted in principal's meetings being canceled to accommodate the cluster meetings. Eventually, Mr. Stern started to countermand cluster invitations to "his" teachers. His shout,

"I am still your boss," echoes in the ears of many. His parting words to Rita and the cluster staff were "We'll see how long you last!"

DIAGNOSTIC DEBRIEF

Here are some questions that can be used to assess an institution's ability to change:

- Are all the steps of the integrated change model being implemented?
- Is a force-field analysis used during the change process?
- Are the intervention strategies appropriate for the situation?
- Do mechanisms exist for institutionalizing the change?

Chapter 11

Leading with Heart

Everybody has a calling. And your real job in life is to figure out as soon as possible what that is, who you were meant to be, and to begin to honor that in the best way possible for yourself.

—*Oprah Winfrey*

How the leader utilizes the concepts contained in the preceding chapters of this book depends largely on their philosophy of life regarding how human beings behave in the workplace. The two extremes of the continuum might be described as those leaders who believe that human beings are basically lazy and will do the very least that they need to do to "get by" in the workplace. Or those who believe that people are basically industrious and, if given the choice, would opt for doing a quality job.

It would seem that today's most effective leaders hold the latter view. Max DePree, former owner and CEO of the highly successful Herman Miller Furniture Company, writes in his book *Leadership Is an Art*, that a leader's function is to "liberate people to do what is required of them in the most effective and humane way possible" (DePree, 1989). Instead of catching people doing something wrong, the goal as enlightened leaders is to catch them doing something right. It is suggested, therefore, that in addition to a rational approach to leadership (leading with *mind)*, a truly enlightened leader leads with heart.

Too often, leaders underestimate the skills and qualities of their followers. Consider the story of Bill Faries, the chief custodian at a high school. Bill's mother, with whom he had been extraordinarily close, had passed away after a long illness. The school was religiously affiliated and the school community went "all out" in its remembrance of Bill's mother. They held a religious service in which almost 3,000 members of the school community participated. As a token of Bill's gratitude he gave the school a six-by-eight-foot knitted quilt that he had personally sewn. From that point on, Bill was no longer viewed as just a custodian. He encompassed two identities; he was both a custodian and a story teller through quilt making. The point is that it took the death of his mother for others to realize how truly talented Bill was outside of his custodian duties.

The previous story supports that the effectiveness of leadership begins with an understanding of the diversity of people's gifts, talents, and skills. When thinking about the variety of gifts that people bring to organizations and institutions, one may come to see that leading with heart lies in cultivating, liberating, and enabling those gifts.

LEADERSHIP DEFINED

The first responsibility of a leader is to define reality through a vision. The last is to say "thank you." In between, the leader must become the servant of the servants. Being a leader means having the opportunity to make a meaningful difference in the lives of those who allow leaders to lead. To summarize, leaders who lead with heart do not inflict pain; they bear pain.

Whether one is a successful leader can be determined by looking at the followers. Are they reaching their potential? Are they learning? Are they able to change without bitterness? Are they able to achieve the institution's goals and objectives? Can they manage conflict among themselves? Leading with heart resides where the answers to these questions is an emphatic "yes."

Can leadership be considered in terms of what the gospel writer Luke calls, the "one who serves"? The leader owes something to the institution they lead. The leader is seen in this context as steward rather than owner or proprietor. Leading with heart requires the leader to think about their stewardship in terms of legacy, direction, effectiveness, and values.

Legacy

Too many of today's leaders are interested only in immediate results that bolster their career goals. Long-range goals are left to their successors. It is believed this approach fosters autocratic leadership, which oftentimes produces short-term results but militates against creativity and its long-term benefits. In effect, this approach is the antithesis of leading with heart.

On the contrary, leaders should build a long-lasting legacy of accomplishment that is institutionalized for posterity. They owe their institutions and their followers a healthy existence and the relationships and reputation that enable continuity of that healthy existence. Leaders are also responsible for future leadership succession. They need to identify, develop, and nurture future leaders to carry on the legacy.

Values

Along with being responsible for providing future leaders, leaders owe the individuals in their institution certain other legacies. Leaders need to be concerned with the institutional value system that determines the principles and standards that guide the practices of those in the organization. Leaders need to model their value systems so that the individuals in the organization can learn to transmit these values to their colleagues and to future employees. In a civilized institution, visible display of good manners, respect for people, and an appreciation of the way in which people serve matter. A humane, sensitive, and thoughtful leader will transmit their value system through their daily behavior.

Direction

Leaders are obliged to provide and maintain direction by developing a vision. The point was made earlier that effective leaders must leave their organizations with a legacy. Part of this legacy should be a sense of progress or momentum. An educational administrator, for instance, should imbue his or her institution with a sense on continuous progress—a sense of constant improvement.

Improvement and momentum come from a clear vision of what the institution ought to be, from a well-planned strategy to achieve that vision, and from carefully developed and articulated directions and plans that allow everyone to participate and feel personally accountable for achieving those plans.

Effectiveness

Leaders are also responsible for effectiveness by being enablers. They need to enable others to reach their potential both personally and institutionally. The most effective ways of enabling one's colleagues is through participative decision-making. It begins with believing in the potential of people—believing in their diversity of gifts.

Leaders must realize that to maximize their own power and effectiveness, they need to empower others. Leaders are responsible for setting and attaining the goals in their organizations. Empowering or enabling others to help achieve those goals enhances the leader's chances of attaining those goals, ultimately enhancing the leader's effectiveness and power. Paradoxically, giving up power really amounts to gaining power.

Chapter 11

IT STARTS WITH TRUST AND RESPECT

These are exciting times in education. Revolutionary steps are being taken to restructure schools and rethink the teaching-learning process. The concepts of empowerment, total quality management, the use of technology, and strategic planning are becoming the norm. However, although these activities have the potential to influence education in significantly positive ways, they must be based upon a strong foundation to achieve their full potential.

Achieving educational effectiveness is an incremental, sequential improvement process. This improvement process begins by building a sense of security within each individual so that he or she can be flexible in adapting to changes within education. Addressing only skills or techniques, such as communication, motivation, negotiation, or empowerment, is ineffective when individuals in an organization do not trust its systems, themselves, or each other. An institution's resources are wasted when invested only in training programs that assist teacher and staff in mastering quick-fix techniques that at best attempt to manipulate and at worst reinforce mistrust.

The challenge is to transform relationships based on insecurity, adversity, and politics to those based on mutual trust. Trust is the beginning of effectiveness and forms the foundation of a principle-centered learning environment that places emphasis upon strengths and devises innovative methods to minimize weaknesses. The transformation process requires an internal locus of control that emphasizes individual responsibility and accountability for change and for promoting effectiveness.

TEAMWORK

For many, there exists a dichotomy between how one sees themself as a person and how they see themself as a worker. Chapter 1 of this book contains the following words of a Zen Buddhist:

The master in the art of living makes little distinction
between his work and his play, his labor and his leisure,
his mind and his body, his education and his recreation,
his love and his religion. He hardly knows which is which.
 He simply pursues his vision of excellence in whatever he does,
 leaving others to decide whether he is working or playing.
 To him he is always doing both.

Work can be and should be productive, rewarding, enriching, fulfilling, and joyful. Work is a great privilege, and it is up to leaders to make certain that work is everything that it can and should be.

Paramount among the ideals that leaders need to recognize in leading an organization is the notion of teamwork and the valuing of each individual's contribution to the final product. The synergy produced by an effective team is greater than the sum of its parts.

The foundation of the team is the recognition that each member needs every other member and no individual can be successful without the cooperation of others. Consider the story of a young boy, who was a very enthusiastic baseball fan. The boy's favorite player was the Hall of Fame pitcher Robin Roberts of the Philadelphia Phillies. During the early 1950s, Roberts's fastball dominated the National League. The boy's uncle, who took him to his first ballgame, explained that opposing batters were so intimidated by Roberts's fastball that they were automatic "outs" even before they got to the plate. The uncle claimed that Robin Roberts was unstoppable. But the young boy questioned this logic, for he knew that no one was unstoppable by oneself. The boy retorted to his uncle that he knew how to stop Robin Roberts. "Make me his catcher!" he excitedly proclaimed.

EMPLOYEES AS VOLUNTEERS

Institutions will not amount to anything without the people who make them what they are. And the individuals most influential in this task are essentially volunteers. The very best employees can work anywhere they please. So, in a sense, they volunteer to work where they do. It could be said that leaders would do far better if they looked upon and treated employees as volunteers. This point was made earlier in that leaders should treat employees through a covenantal rather than a contractual relationship.

Alexander Solzhenitsyn, speaking to the 1978 graduating class of Harvard College, said this about legalistic relationships:

> a society based on the letter of the law and never reaching any higher, fails to take advantage of the full range of human possibilities. The letter of the law is too cold and formal to have a beneficial influence on society. Whenever the tissue of life is woven of legalistic relationships, this creates an atmosphere of spiritual mediocrity that paralyzes men's noblest impulses.

And later: "After a certain level of the problem has been reached, legalistic thinking induces paralysis; it prevents one from seeing the scale and the meaning of events" (Solzhenitsyn, 1978).

Covenantal relationships, on the other hand, induce freedom, not paralysis. As the noted psychiatrist William Glasser explains, "coercion only produces mediocrity; love or a sense of belonging produces excellence" (Glasser, 1984). The goal as leaders is to encourage a covenantal relationship of love, warmth, and personal chemistry among employee volunteers. Shared ideals, shared goals, shared respect, a sense of integrity, a sense of quality, a sense of advocacy, and a sense of caring are the basis of an organization's covenant with its employees.

EMPLOYEE OWNERS

If an educational institution is to be successful, everyone in it needs to feel that they own the place. Educators should retort, "This is not the school district's school; it is not the school board's school; it is my school!" Taking ownership is a sign of one's love for an institution. In his book *Servant Leadership*, Robert Greenleaf says, "Love is an indefinable term, and its manifestations are both subtle and infinite. It has only one absolute condition: unlimited liability!" Although it might run counter to traditional notion of American capitalism, employees should be encouraged to act as if they own the place. It is a sign of love (Greenleaf, 2008).

IMPLICATIONS FOR PRACTICE: LEADING WITH HEART CASE STUDY

St. Anthony Academy (SAA) is a private school for children in preschool through grade eight that is owned and operated by a religious congregation. The board of directors for SAA consists of the seven members of the leadership team for the religious congregation. The principal and vice principal are directly accountable to the board. In addition to principal and vice principal, the administrative team for the school consists of the treasurer, the director of admissions, the director of religious education, the director of development and alumni relations, director of information communication and technology, and the director of public relations. This team is supported by an administrative assistant and two school secretaries.

A year ago, Ms. Love was selected from a pool of external candidates to be the new principal at SAA. At that time, a vice principal was also selected from among its faculty leadership. The person selected, Mr. Stem, had been a respected teacher at SAA for seven years.

The principal came with the experience of being principal in two other schools, whereas Mr. Stem had the experience of being a teacher and the director of admissions in this school, so he knew what needed to be changed in the school. Still, Ms. Love was "new" and not known, making it easier for people to accept change, as one is usually more gracious at expecting change when a new leader is named. Fortunately, SAA was already a very good school; this new leadership team was tasked with making it better.

SAA had just completed their Middle States evaluation so it was known what needed to be done, and the school community was ready for the work. It was relatively easy for this new leadership team to be *agents of change*. Ms. Love and Mr. Stem developed a five-year action plan to implement. This plan was developed over the previous spring and summer with input from the board, teachers and administrative team, and parents. This plan gave form to a new, revised vision for the school. The vision was communicated widely to the larger community and helped initiate institutional changes.

To motivate teachers to continually embrace change, SAA leaders implemented a process model called goal-setting theory. Each year, teachers set goals and school leadership works with them to develop those goals over the course of the year. Teacher evaluation at the end of the year reflects their success at reaching their goals, although many times these goals are in-process from one year to the next. Some years, teachers are asked to set goal in relation to a schoolwide theme. For example, this year, since the strategic plan was presented to the faculty and staff in September, employees set their personal goals around the implementation of the strategic plan goals for the school. For teachers, formal observations in the classroom asked teachers to demonstrate, where possible, how they are implementing these goals.

Ms. Love happens to be very non-confrontational. When she did make decisions, she did so with a priority given to others and the impact that decision might have on their life. Mr. Stem tends to want to jump right in and fix things that are perceived as broken. He also employs a decision-making process wherein logic and concrete rational prevail.

The use of different styles of dealing with conflict began to create a rift between the dynamic leadership duo. While both liked to verbally profess a belief in collaboration, their actions didn't always support this approach. Given the structure of communication within the school and responsibility that they had to meet together in grade teams or with the total faculty, the need to present a more united front was necessary.

DIAGNOSTIC DEBRIEF

If the following conditions are prevalent in an institution, the leaders are most likely **not leading with heart**:

- when there is a tendency to merely "go through the motions";
- when a dark tension exits among key individuals or groups and cynical attitude prevail;

- when finding time to celebrate accomplishments becomes problematic;
- when stories and storytellers are nowhere to be found;
- when there is the view that one person's gain needs to be at another's expense;
- when leaders accumulate power rather than share it;
- when attainment of short-term goals is preferred to the acquisition on long-term goals;
- when educators treat students as impositions;
- when the accidents become more important than the essence;
- when the loss of grace, style, and civility occur;
- when leaders use coercion to motivate employees;
- when administrators dwell on individuals' weaknesses rather than their strengths;
- when diversity and individual charisms are not respected.

Chapter 12

What Have We Learned?

The greatest discovery of my generation is that man can alter his life simply by altering his attitude of mind.

—William James

INTRODUCTION

What has been learned about organizational development and leadership in the last eleven chapters of this book? First, readership learned a systematic way of diagnosing an institution's organization health, namely, by constantly assessing the eleven components of an organization. Secondly, readers gained the knowledge and skills to address many weaknesses found in school organizations and leadership in general.

Situational or contingency leadership theory as a solid grounded approach was also discovered. Today's leaders and aspiring leaders need to be able to adapt their leadership behavior to changing situations. No one can afford to be "stuck" in one paradigm. The truly heroic leaders are successful because they are able to very effectively balance their use of the four leadership frames enunciated by Lee Bolman and Terrence Deal, while filtering all of one's leadership behavior through a moral frame. Finally, readership learned the importance of organizational development and leadership *theory*.

THE IMPORTANCE OF THEORY

We cannot underestimate the value and importance of theory in the field of organizational development and leadership, or in any other field for that matter. Without theory there would be no valid way of diagnosing, analyzing, and correcting failed practice. Without a theoretical base, one is left to risk leading by trial and error, or by the proverbial "seat of your pants."

Theory is to leadership as the fundamentals are to athletics. For example, if a basketball player is suddenly shooting a lower percentage than their career average, something is obviously wrong. They have experienced "failed practice." What to do?

Most athletes in this situation are coached to "go back to the basics or the fundamentals." The basketball player will review the fundamentals of shooting, like squaring oneself to the basket, keeping the shooting elbow in, keeping the guide-hand off the ball upon release, snapping the wrist, and exaggerating one's follow-through. It is likely that one or more of these fundamentals is being violated and causing the shooting percentage decline and when corrected, the percentage will rise again to its most recent average.

If the athlete does not know the fundamentals of shooting, also termed *shooting theory,* they can only correct the problem through the very inefficient means of trial and error. The same goes for leaders who are losing their impact on their followers. If they have not adopted a leadership theory to guide their behavior, they can only correct the leadership decline by trial and error.

However, if the leader has internalized a leadership theory, the leader can review the tenets or principles of the theory and most likely diagnose the deficiency and correct it rather quickly. For example, the leader might find that their followers are no longer responding to the leader's friendly persuasion and active support (human resource leadership behavior).

In analyzing the previous *situation*, the leader might conclude that they are using human resource behavior with the followers when structural leadership behavior may be more appropriate. As a result of this analysis, the leader may decide to utilize a more structural approach and "lay down the law" to his recalcitrant followers. This rather simple example demonstrates the importance and value of theory in providing leaders with the knowledge and skills they need to be able to diagnose and correct failed practice in an efficient and effective way.

LEADING WITH MIND

Knowledge of one's field is a sine qua non for effective leadership. This quality usually manifests itself in one's structural frame leadership behavior.

In sports terms, the leader must have a good command of the fundamentals of the game. In business terms, the effective leader must have a thorough knowledge of the technical aspects of how a business operates and a sense of how to develop a viable business plan. In education, the leader needs to know how schools and school systems operate and what the best practices in the field are in curriculum and instruction. In a family situation, the leader (parent or guardian) needs to have at least a modicum of knowledge regarding the principles of child psychology. In short, leaders in any field need to know that field and be able to apply that knowledge through the theory and practice of organizational development which would include the following:

a. Organizational structure: how an institution is organized.
b. Organizational culture: the values and beliefs of an institution.
c. Motivation: the system of rewards and incentives provided.
d. Communication: the clarity and accuracy of the communication process.
e. Decision-making: how and by whom decisions are made.
f. Conflict management: how dysfunctional conflict is handled.
g. Power distribution: how the power in an institution is distributed.
h. Strategic planning: how the mission, vision, and strategic plan are developed.
i. Change: how change is effectively implemented in an institution.
j. Leading with heart: whether a culture of trust and respect prevails in an institution.

Included in the Appendix is a pair of diagnostic tools entitled "The Heart Smart Survey I and II" which I developed to help leaders assess the organizational health of their institutions. Heart Smart I assesses whether the leaders are leading with *mind*, and Heart Smart II assesses whether the leaders are leading with *heart*. Together they identify which of the factors listed earlier need improvement.

LEADING WITH HEART

To recap, then, the effective leader needs to be *technically* competent. However, being technically competent is not enough. To be truly effective and heroic, leaders need to master the *art* of leadership and learn to lead with *heart*. In effect, leaders need to operate out of both the structural and political frames (science) and the human resources, symbolic, and moral frames (art) to maximize their effectiveness. This means that they must be concerned about the person (cura personalis). They must abide by the golden rule and treat others as they wish to be treated. As noted earlier, truly effective leaders treat their employees like volunteers and empower them to actualize their true potential, thus engendering mutual trust and respect among their colleagues.

In their book entitled *Leading with Kindness* (2008), William Baker and Michael O'Malley reiterate the views expressed in this book. They explore how one of the most unheralded features of leadership, that is basic human kindness, drives successful organizations. And while most scholars generally recognize that a leader's emotional intelligence factors into that person's leadership behavior, most are reticent to consider it to be as important as analytical ability, decision-making skills, or implementation skills. Such emotions as compassion, empathy, and kindness are often dismissed as unquantifiable, and are often seen as weaknesses. Yet, research in neuroscience and the social sciences clearly reveals that one's physiological and emotional states have measurable effects on both individual and group performance.

In the jargon of the day, individuals who lead with heart or kindness are said to have a high degree of emotional intelligence. Many are familiar with the current notion of multiple intelligences: that is, individuals have a number of intelligences in addition to cognitive intelligence. Among these intelligences is emotional intelligence. Several theories within the emotional intelligence paradigm seek to understand how individuals perceive, understand, utilize, and manage emotions in an effort to predict and foster personal effectiveness.

Most of these models define emotional intelligence as an array of traits and abilities related to emotional and social knowledge that influence an overall ability to effectively cope with environmental demands; as such, it can be viewed as a model of psychological well-being and adaptation. This includes the ability to be aware of, to understand, and to relate to others; the ability to deal with strong emotions and to control one's impulses; and the ability to adapt to change and to solve problems of a personal and social nature.

The five main domains of emotional intelligence models are intrapersonal skills, interpersonal skills, adaptability, stress management, and general mood. If the reader sees a similarity between emotional intelligence and what is being termed *leading with heart* and what Baker and O'Malley call *leading with kindness*, it is not coincidental.

LEADING WITH MIND AND HEART

So, the truly heroic leaders lead with *both* mind (science) and heart (art)—with cognitive intelligence and emotional intelligence. One or the other will not suffice. Only by mastering both will the leader succeed. For example, former president Donald Trump was rendered ineffective as a leader because of his tenacious push to share inaccurate and unsubstantiated claims of widespread voter fraud, which led to the January 2021 insurrection on Capitol Hill by pro-Trump supporters. Why was he deemed ineffective? Because he suddenly lost the *knowledge* of how government works (science)? No! He lost his ability to lead because he lost the *trust and respect* of much of the American public (art). He could still lead with his mind, but he had lost the ability to lead with heart. It remains to be determined how long it will take for him to reestablishing his integrity with the American public.

On the contrary, one could argue that former president Jimmie Carter lost his ability to lead because of a perceived lack of competency. Rightly or wrongly, the majority of the voting public did not believe that he had the knowledge necessary to manage government operations and effectively lead with mind. However, virtually no one questioned his concern for people, his integrity, and his ability to lead with heart. Absent the perceived ability to do *both*, however, he lost the 1980 election to Ronald Reagan.

We conclude, then, that effective leaders are situational; that is, they are capable of adapting their leadership behavior to the situation. They utilize structural, human resources, symbolic, political, and moral leadership behavior, when appropriate. They lead with both mind (structural and political behavior) and with heart (human resources, symbolic, and moral behavior). They master both the science (mind) and art (heart) of leadership, and in doing so, they are transformational, leading their organizations to new heights. As Chris Lowney (2003) writes in *Heroic Leadership*, such leaders are, in a word, truly "heroic."

CONCLUSION

What has been attempted in this book is to provide a "go to" guide for aligning mind and heart in leadership and organization dynamics. Each chapter presents key components to ensure success for school leaders, as they strive to be effective agents of change. Together, the topics offered herein seek to provide foundational theory to support practice in the field. These components work in tandem to ensure effective school management, where teachers feel supported in creating a learning environment where all students thrive.

Appendix
Heart Smart Surveys I and II

Just as there are vital signs in measuring individual health, it is believed that there are vital signs for measuring the health of educational institutions. This survey (Heart Smart Survey I) will help to identify those vital signs in your school or school system. It, along with Heart Smart Survey II, will indicate further whether the institution's leaders are leading with both mind and heart.

HEART SMART SURVEY I

Please think of your *present work environment* and indicate the degree to which you disagree or agree with each of the following statements. A "1" is *strongly disagree* and a "7" is *strongly agree*.

Strongly Disagree	Disagree	Slightly Disagree	Neither Disagree nor Agree	Slightly Agree	Agree	Strongly Agree
1	2	3	4	5	6	7

1. The manner in which the tasks in this institution are divided is a logical one.
2. The relationships among coworkers are harmonious.
3. The institution's leadership efforts result in its fulfillment of its purposes.
4. My work at this institution offers me an opportunity to grow as a person.
5. I can always talk to someone at work, if I have a work-related problem.
6. The faculty actively participates in decisions.
7. There is little evidence of unresolved conflict in this institution.

8. There is a strong fit between this institution's mission and my own values.
9. The faculty and staff are represented on most committees and task forces.
10. Staff development routinely accompanies any significant changes that occur in this institution.
11. The manner in which the tasks in this institution are distributed is a fair one.
12. Older faculty's opinions are valued.
13. The administrators display the behaviors required for effective leadership.
14. The rewards and incentives here are both internal and external.
15. There is open and direct communication among all levels of this institution.
16. Participative decision-making is fostered at this institution.
17. What little conflict that exists at this institution is not dysfunctional.
18. Representatives of all segments of the school community participate in the strategic planning process.
19. The faculty and staff have an appropriate voice in the operation of this institution.
20. This institution is not resistant to constructive change.
21. The division of labor in this organization helps its efforts to reach its goals.
22. I feel valued by this institution.
23. The administration encourages an appropriate amount of participation in decision-making.
24. Faculty and staff members are often recognized for special achievements.
25. There are no significant barriers to effective communication at this institution.
26. When the *acceptance* of a decision is important, a group decision-making model is used.
27. There are mechanisms at this institution to effectively manage conflict and stress.
28. Most of the employees understand the mission and goals of this institution.
29. The faculty and staff feel empowered to make their own decisions regarding their daily work.
30. Tolerance toward change is modeled by the administration of this institution.
31. The various grade level teachers and departments work well together.
32. Differences among people are accepted.
33. The leadership is able to generate continuous improvement in the institution.
34. My ideas are encouraged, recognized, and used.

35. Communication is carried out in a nonaggressive style.
36. In general, the decision-making process is an effective one.
37. Conflicts are usually resolved before they become dysfunctional.
38. For the most part, the employees of this institution feel an "ownership" of its goals.
39. The faculty and staff are encouraged to be creative in their work.
40. When changes are made they do so within a rational process.
41. This institution's organizational design responds well to changes in the internal and external environment.
42. The teaching and the nonteaching staffs get along with one another.
43. The leadership of this institution espouses a clear educational vision.
44. The goals and objectives for the year are mutually developed by the faculty and the administration.
45. I believe that my opinions and ideas are listened to.
46. Usually, a collaborative style of decision-making is utilized at this institution.
47. A collaborative approach to conflict resolution is ordinarily used.
48. This institution has a clear educational vision.
49. The faculty and staff can express their opinions without fear of retribution.
50. I feel confident that I will have an opportunity for input if a significant change were to take place in this institution.
51. This institution is "people-oriented."
52. Administrators and faculty have mutual respect for one another.
53. Administrators give people the freedom to do their job.
54. The rewards and incentives in this institution are designed to satisfy a variety of individual needs.
55. The opportunity for feedback is always available in the communications process.
56. Group decision-making techniques, like brainstorming and group surveys are sometimes used in the decision-making process.
57. Conflicts are oftentimes prevented by early intervention.
58. This institution has a strategic plan for the future.
59. Most administrators here use the power of persuasion rather than the power of coercion.
60. This institution is committed to continually improving through the process of change.
61. This institution does not adhere to a strict chain of command.
62. This institution exhibits grace, style, and civility.
63. The administrators model desired behavior.
64. At this institution, employees are not normally coerced into doing things.
65. I have the information that I need to do a good job.

66. I can constructively challenge the decisions in this institution.
67. A process to resolve work-related grievances is available.
68. There is an ongoing planning process at this institution.
69. The faculty and staff have input into the operation of this institution through a collective bargaining unit or through a faculty governance body.
70. The policies, procedures, and programs of this institution are periodically reviewed.

Instructions: Transfer the numbers you circled on the questionnaire to the blanks below. Add each column and divide each sum by seven. This will give you comparable scores for each of the ten areas.

	S	C	L	M	CO	D	CR	G	P	A
	1.___	2.___	3.___	4.___	5.___	6.___	7.___	8.___	9.___	10.___
	11.___	12.___	13.___	14.___	15.___	16.___	17.___	18.___	19.___	20.___
	21.___	22.___	23.___	24.___	25.___	26.___	27.___	28.___	29.___	30.___
	31.___	32.___	33.___	34.___	35.___	36.___	37.___	38.___	39.___	40.___
	41.___	42.___	43.___	44.___	45.___	46.___	47.___	48.___	49.___	50.___
	51.___	52.___	53.___	54.___	55.___	56.___	57.___	58.___	59.___	60.___
	61.___	62.___	63.___	64.___	66.___	66.___	67.___	68.___	69.___	70.___
Total										
Average										

HEART SMART I—SCORE CARD LEGEND

S = structure, C = culture, L = leadership, M = motivation, CO = communication, D = decision-making, CR = conflict resolution, G = goal setting/planning, P = power distribution, A = attitude toward change

INTERPRETATION SHEET (HEART SMART I)

Instructions: Transfer your average scores from the Scoring Sheet to the appropriate boxes. Then study the background information and interpretation suggestions that follow.

Background

Heart Smart Organizational Diagnosis Questionnaire is a survey-feedback instrument designed to collect data on organizational functioning. It measures the perceptions of persons in an organization to determine areas of activity that would benefit from an organizational development effort. It can be used as the sole data-collection technique or in conjunction with other techniques (interview, observation, etc.). The instrument and the model reflect a systematic approach for analyzing relationships among variables that influence how an organization is managed. Using the Heart Smart Organizational Diagnosis Questionnaire is the first step in determining appropriate interventions for organizational change efforts.

Interpretation and Diagnosis

A crucial consideration is the diagnosis based upon data interpretation. The simplest diagnosis would be to assess the amount of variance for each of the ten variables in relation to a score of 4, which is the neutral point. Scores *below* 4 would indicate a *problem* with organizational functioning. The closer the score is to 1, the more severe the problem would be. Scores *above* 4 indicate the *lack of a problem*, with a score of 7 indicating optimum functioning.

Another diagnostic approach follows the same guidelines of assessment in relation to the neutral point (score) of 4. The score of each of the seventy items on the questionnaire can be reviewed to produce more exacting information on problematic areas. Thus, diagnosis would be more precise. For example, let us suppose that the average score on item number 8 is 1.4. This would indicate not only a problem in organizational purpose or goal-setting but also a more specific problem in that there is a gap between organizational and individual goals. This more precise diagnostic effort is likely to lead to a more appropriate intervention in the organization than the generalized diagnostic approach described in the preceding paragraph.

Appropriate diagnosis must address the relationships between the boxes to determine the interconnectedness of problems. For example, if there is a problem with *communication,* could it be that the organizational *structure* does not foster effective communication? This might be the case if the average score on item 25 was well below 4 (2.5 or lower) and all the items on organizational *structure* (1, 11, 21, 31, 41, 51, 61) also averaged below 4.0.

THE HEART SMART SURVEY II

Please think of your *present work environment* and indicate the degree to which you disagree or agree with each of the following statements. A "1" is *strongly agree* and a "7" is *strongly disagree*.

Strongly Agree	Agree	Slightly Agree	Neither Disagree nor Agree	Slightly Disagree	Disagree	Strongly Disagree
1	2	3	4	5	6	7

1. There is not much evidence of faculty and staff holding and espousing ethical values.
2. There is not much evidence of mutual respect and understanding among the faculty and staff.
3. There is not much of a sense of voluntarism and dedication among the teachers and staff.
4. There is not much indication that teachers and staff have committed themselves to the modeling of moral and ethical values.
5. There is not much trust and respect shared among faculty, staff, and administration.
6. There is little evidence that teachers encourage students to be concerned for the underserved in their communities.
7. There is not much evidence that the teachers are supportive of a moral or ethical code to guide one's behavior.
8. There are not many occasions when the faculty and staff get to interact with one another.
9. There are not many opportunities presented to students to develop an appreciation of and respect for cultures other than their own.
10. Teachers do not often bear witness to their values and beliefs through their daily behavior.
11. The faculty and staff do not seem to support one another in various events and activities.
12. There are not many occasions when faculty members accompany their students on community service activities.
13. There are no occasions when faculty and students discuss their values and beliefs.

14. There is not much in the way of promotion of justice and fairness among students.
15. There is not a culture that fosters service to the community at this institution.
16. The faculty does not seem to go out of its way to model their belief system to the students.
17. There is not much evidence of the promotion of justice and fairness among teachers.
18. There are not many occasions when teachers engage in community service by donating space, time, resources, and personal help.
19. There are not many times when the faculty and staff articulate or speak out on their values and beliefs.
20. There is not much evidence of the promotion of justice and fairness between teachers and administrators.
21. There are not many instances of faculty evidencing compassion and giving service to the needy, the disadvantaged, and troubled students and coworkers.
22. There are not many occasions when the faculty discusses teaching values and ethics.
23. There are significant barriers to effective communication at this institution.
24. The overall morale of the school is not very good.
25. The faculty and staff do not show much concern for world problems, like hunger, poverty, war, pollution, and social justice.
26. The faculty does not openly express its support of ethical and moral values.
27. The conflicts that arise among individuals and groups are not resolved very well.
28. The teachers do not encourage a sense of service and social justice in their students very much.
29. The faculty do not avail themselves of professional development opportunities to develop their skills in teaching values education.
30. The sense of trust and respect at this institution is not very high.
31. There is a tendency to merely "go through the motions" at this school.
32. There is a tendency for the superficial to be more important than the substantial at this school.
33. There is a dark tension that exists among key individuals at this school.

34. It seems that the attainment of short-term goals is preferred to the achievement of long-term goals.
35. There seems to be a loss of grace, style, and civility at this institution.
36. There is a tendency to do the minimal and not "go the extra yard" at this school.
37. The administration seems to use coercion to motivate employees here.
38. We do not ever seem to be able to find the time to celebrate accomplishments here.
39. The teachers and staff seem to treat students like customers or impositions here.
40. The employees feel manipulated and exploited here.
41. There don't seem to be many stories and storytellers to carry on the tradition at this school.
42. The leaders here seem to want to be served rather than to serve.
43. There seems to be a certain arrogance among the leaders at this school.
44. There seems to be a sense of competition here whereby one person or group's gain always has to be at another's expense.
45. Teachers here won't pick up a piece of paper because "that's the janitor's job."
46. When something goes wrong here, there is a tendency to want to cast blame.
47. Diversity and individual charisma are not respected here.
48. Teachers here seem to use up all their sick days even if they are not sick.
49. The administration seems to accumulate power rather than sharing it at this institution.
50. The climate in this school seems to encourage competition rather than collaboration.
51. Teachers seem to work solely for a paycheck here.
52. Teachers are asked to teach to the test to improve test scores at this school.
53. There is a tendency for the faculty rooms to be sources of malicious gossip and rumors.
54. There is a union mentality here whereby teachers do not want to do anything extra unless they are paid.
55. Administrators here seem to dwell on people's weaknesses rather than their strengths.
56. Individual turf is protected to the detriment of institutional goals at this school.

57. There is definitely a caste system here among the administration, the faculty, and the clerical and custodian staffs.

Instructions: Transfer the numbers you circled on the questionnaire to the blanks below. Add each column and divide each sum by 19. This will give you comparable scores for each of the three areas.

More Integrity	**Community**	**Service/Social Justice**
1.___	2.___	3.___
4.___	5.___	6.___
7.___	8.___	9.___
10.___	11.___	12.___
13.___	14.___	15.___
16.___	17.___	18.___
19.___	20.___	21.___
22.___	23.___	24.___
25___	26.___	27.___
28.___	29.___	30.___
31.___	32.___	33.___
34.___	35.___	36.___
37.___	38.___	39.___
40.___	41.___	42.___
43.___	44.___	45.___

More Integrity	Community	Service/Social Justice
46.___	47.___	48.___
49.___	50.___	51.___
52.___	53.___	54.___
55.___	56.___	57.___
Total		
Average (sum score divided by 19)		

INTERPRETATION SHEET (HEART SMART II)

Instructions: Study the background information and interpretation suggestions that follow.

Background

Heart Smart Organizational Diagnosis Questionnaires are survey-feedback instruments designed to collect data on organizational functioning. They measure the perceptions of persons in an organization to determine areas of activity that would benefit from an organizational development effort. It can be used as the sole data-collection technique or in conjunction with other techniques (interview, observation, and so forth). The instrument and the model reflect a systematic approach for analyzing relationships among variables that influence how an organization is managed. Using the Heart Smart Organizational Diagnosis Questionnaires is the first step in determining appropriate interventions for organizational change efforts.

Interpretation and Diagnosis

A crucial consideration is the diagnosis based upon data interpretation. The simplest diagnosis would be to assess the amount of variance for each of the three variables in relation to a score of 4, which is the neutral point. Scores *below* 4 would indicate a problem with organizational functioning. The closer the score is to 1, the more severe the problem would be. Scores *above* 4 indicate the *lack of a problem*, with a score of 7 indicating optimum functioning.

Another diagnostic approach follows the same guidelines of assessment in relation to the neutral point (score) of 4. The score of each of the fifty-seven items on the questionnaire can be reviewed to produce more exacting information on problematic areas. Thus, diagnosis would be more precise. For example, let us suppose that the average score on item number 8 is 2.4. This would indicate not only a problem in the sense of community in the institution but also a more specific problem in that there are not enough occasions provided for the teachers to interact with one another. This more precise diagnostic effort is likely to lead to a more appropriate intervention in the organization than the generalized diagnostic approach described in the preceding paragraph.

HEART SMART ORGANIZATION DIAGNOSIS QUESTIONNAIRES

Just as there are vital signs in measuring individual health, we believe that there are vital signs in measuring the good health of organizations. These surveys will help us to identify those vital signs in your school or school system. The purpose of the Heart Smart Organizational Diagnosis Questionnaires, therefore, is to provide feedback data for intensive diagnostic efforts. Use of the questionnaire, either by itself or in conjunction with other information-collecting techniques such as systematic observation or interviewing, will provide the data needed for identifying strengths and weaknesses in the functioning of an educational institution, and help determine whether the leaders are leading with both mind and heart.

A meaningful diagnostic effort must be based on a theory or model of organizational development. This makes action research possible as it facilitates problem identification, which is essential to determining the proper functioning of an organization. The model suggested here establishes a systematic approach for analyzing relationships among the variables that influence how an organization is managed. Heart Smart Survey I provides for assessment in ten areas of formal and informal activity (see *Heart Smart Wheel Diagram*). Heart Smart Survey II provides for assessment of three areas of formal and informal activity: moral integrity, a sense of community, and a dedication to service and social justice. The outer periphery in the following diagram represents an organizational boundary for diagnosis. This boundary demarcates the functioning of the internal and external environments. Since the underlying organizational theory upon which this survey is based is an open-systems model, it is essential that influences from both the internal and external environment be considered for the analysis to be complete.

THE HEART SMART WHEEL DIAGRAM

Structure
How is this institution organized?

Conflict Resolution	**Culture**
Is the institution functional or dysfunctional?	What values and beliefs are important here?
Goal Setting and Planning	**Leadership**
Are the goals clear, accepted, and operationalized?	How effectively are the boxes kept in balance?
INTERNAL	**ENVIRONMENT**
Power Distribution	**Motivation**
Are the faculty and staff empowered?	Are the rewards and incentives effective?
Attitude	**Communication**
Is the institution continually improving?	Is the message being transmitted clearly?

Decision-Making
How and by whom are decisions being made?

Internal Environment	**External Environment**

References

Adams, J.L. 1986. *The Care and Feeding of Ideas: A Guide to Encouraging Creativity.* Reading, MA: Addison-Wesley.
Anderson, M. 2017. "Transformational Leadership in Education: A Review of Existing Literature," *International Social Science Review, 93*(1), 1–13.
Ärlestig, H. 2008. "In School Communication: Developing a Pedagogically Focused School Culture," *Values and Ethics in Educational Administration, 7*(1), 1–8.
Arneson, S. 2015. "Improving Teaching, One Conversation at a Time," *Educational Leadership, 72*(7), 32–36.
Baker, W., and O'Malley, M. 2008. *Leading with Kindness.* New York: AMACOM.
Bandura, A. 1978. *Social Learning Theory.* Englewood Cliffs, NJ: Prentice-Hall.
Bolman, L.G., and Deal, T.E. 1991. *Reframing Organizations: Artistry, Choice, and Leadership.* San Francisco, CA: Jossey-Bass.
Blanchard, K., and Johnson, S. 1982. *One Minute Manager.* New York: William Morrow & Company.
Brodsky, S.L. 1988. *The Psychology of Adjustment and Well-being.* New York: Holt, Rinehart and Winston.
Carlson, R. 1990. "Conscious Mental Episodes and Skill Acquisition," *Behavioral and Brain Sciences, 13*, 599.
Chapple, C. 1993. *The Jesuit Tradition in Education and Missions.* Scranton: University of Scranton Press.
DePree, M. 1989. *Leadership Is an Art.* New York: Dell Publishing.
Deming, W.E. 2000. *Out of Crisis.* Boston, MA: MIT Press.
Drew, C. 2020. *8 Models of Communication Explained.* Retrieved from https://helpfulprofessor.com/communication-models/
Dufresne, R.L., Botto, K., and Steele, E.S. 2015. "Contributing to an Ignatian Perspective on Leadership," *Journal of Jesuit Business Education, 6*, 1–19.
Dweck, C. 2008. *Mindset: How You Can Fulfil Your Potential.* New York: Ballantine Books.

Engle, M., and Gonzalez, J.V. 2014. "Leading and Teaching with Cultural Competence," *Leadership, 44*(2), 34–36.

Fisher, R., and Brown, S. 1988. *Getting Together.* Boston, MA: Houghton-Mifflin.

Fisher, R., and Ury, W. 1981. *Getting to Yes: Negotiating Without Giving In.* Boston, MA: Houghton Mifflin.

Glasser, W. 1984. *Control Theory, a New Explanation of How We Control Our Lives.* New York: Harper & Row.

Goldaber, I. 1984. *The Communication Laboratory: A Collaboration Between Adversaries to Generate Social Change.* Pittsburgh, PA: Pittsburgh Tri-State Area School Study Council, University of Pittsburgh. Also, *The Goldaber Win/Win Contract Development: A Thirty Day Process.* Miami, FL: Center for the Practice of Conflict Management, 1987.

Gordan, J.R. 1993. *A Diagnostic Approach to Organizational Behavior*: Allyn and Bacon.

Greenleaf, R.K. 2008. *The Servant as Leader.* Terre Haute, IN: The Greenleaf Center for Servant Leadership.

Hanson, E.M. 1991. *Educational Administration and Organizational Behavior.* Boston, MA: Allyn and Bacon.

Hart, A.W. 1987. "A Career Ladder's Effect on Teacher Career and Work Attitudes," *American Educational Research Journal, 24*(4), 479–503.

Heilman, M.E., and Stopeck, M.H. 1985. "Being Attractive, Advantage or Disadvantage? Performance Evaluations and Recommended Personnel Actions as a Function of Appearance, Sex, and Job Type," *Organizational Behavior and Human Decision Processes, 35*, 202–215.

Hersey, P., and Blanchard, K.H. 1969. "Life-cycle Theory of Leadership," *Training and Development Journal, 23*, 26–34.

Hersey, P., and Blanchard, K.H. 1988. *Management of Organizational Behavior,* 5th ed. Englewood Cliffs, NJ: Prentice Hall.

Hilton, A., Hilton, G., Dole, S., and Goos, M. 2015. "School Leaders as Participants in Teachers' Professional Development: The Impact on Teachers' and School Leaders' Professional Growth," *Australian Journal of Teacher Education, 40*(12), 104–125.

Huber, G.P. 1980. *Managerial Decision-making.* Glenview, IL: Scott, Foresman; and A. Delbecq, A. Van de Ven, and D. Gustafson, Group Techniques for Program Planning (Glenview, Ill.: Scott, Foresman, 1975), provide an early discussion. See Thomas, J.B. McDaniel, R.R. Jr., and Dooris, M.J. 1989. "Strategic Issue Analysis: NGT + Decision Analysis for Resolving Strategic Issues," *Journal of Applied Behavioral Sciences, 25*(2), 189–200, for more recent examples.

Jones, T.M. 1991. "Ethical Decision-making by Individuals in Organizations: An Issue-Contingent Model," *Academy of Management Review, 16*(2), 366–395.

Kaplan, A. 1964. "Power in Perspective, in Power and Conflict in Organizations," ed. R.L. Kahn and E. Boulding. London: Tavistock.

Kelley, H.H. 1967. "Attribution Theory in Social Psychology," *Nebraska Symposium on Motivation, 14*, 192–241.

Kirkpatrick, S.A., and Locke, E.A. 1991. "Leadership: Do Traits Matter?" *Academy of Management Executive, 5*(2), 49.

Kotter, J.P. 1977. "Power, Dependence, and Effective Management," *Harvard Business Review, 55*, 125–136.

Latham, G.P., and Yukl, G.A. 1975. "A Review of Research on the Application of Goal Setting in Organizations," *Academy of Management Journal, 18*, 824–845.

Lax, D.A., and Sebenius, J.K. 1986. *The Manager as Negotiator*. New York: Free Press.

Lewis, P.V. 1987. *Organizational Communication: The Essence of Effective Management*, 3rd ed. New York: Wiley.

Lowney, C. 2003. *Heroic Leadership*. Chicago: Loyola Press.

Loyola, I. 2007. *The Spiritual Exercises of St. Ignatius of Loyola*. New York: Cosimo Classics.

Maslow, A,H. 1987. *Motivation and Personality*, 3rd ed. New York: Harper & Row.

Meier, D. 2016. "Situational Leadership Theory as a Foundation for a Blended Learning Framework," *Journal of Education and Practice, 7*(10), 25–30.

Michaelsen, L.K., Watson, W.E., and Black, R.H. 1989. "A Realistic Test of Individual vs. Group Consensus Decision-making, *Journal of Applied Psychology, 74*(5), 834–839.

Palestini, R. 2000. *Ten Steps to Educational Reform: Making Change Happen*. Lanham, MD: Rowman & Littlefield Education.

Palestini, R. 2011. *Educational Administration: Leading with Mind and Heart*, 3rd ed. Lanham, MD: Rowman & Littlefield Education.

Palestini, R. 2013. *No Laughing Matter: The Value of Humor in Educational Leadership*. Lanham, MD: Rowman & Littlefield Education.

Pavlov, I. 1927. "Conditioned Reflexes: An Investigation of the Physiological Activity of the Cerebral Cortex," trans. and ed. G.V. Anrep. London: Oxford University Press. Comparable work done in the United States by J.B. Watson is described in *Behaviorism*. (New York: Norton, 1924).

Peters, T., and Waterman, R. 1988. *In Search of Excellence*. New York: Grand Central Publishing.

Polevoi, L. 2012. "Effective Communication Starts with You," *Managing People at Work*, (362), 5.

Rahim, M.A. 1989. "Relationships of Leader Power to Compliance and Satisfaction with Supervision: Evidence from a National Sample of Managers," *Journal of Management, 15*(4), 545–556.

Ravier, A., SJ. 1987, *Ignatius of Loyola and the Founding of the Society of Jesus*. San Francisco, CA: Ignatius Press.

Rest, J.R. 1986. *Moral Development: Advances in Research and Theory* New York: Praeger;

Seaton, F.S. 2018. "Empowering Teachers to Implement a Growth Mindset," *Educational Psychology in Practice, 34*(1), 41–57.

Senge, P.M. 1990. *The Fifth Dimension: The Art of Practice of the Learning Organization*. New York: Doubleday.

Simon, H.A. 1960. *The New Science of Management Decision* New York: Harper.
Solzhenitsyn, A. 1978. *A World Split Apart.* New York: Harper & Row.
Team Leverage Edu (2020). *Modes of Communication.* Retrieved from: https://leverageedu.com/blog/modes-of-communication/
Thorndike, E.L. 1924. *Behaviorism.* New York: Norton; Skinner, B.F. 1938. *The Behavior of Organisms: An Experimental Approach.* New York: Appleton-Century.
Tolman, E.C. 1932. *Purposive Behavior in Animals and Men.* New York: Appleton-Century-Crofts.
Toner, J.J. 1991. *Discerning God's Will: Ignatius of Loyola's Teaching on Christian Decision-making.* St. Louis, MO: The Institute of Jesuit sources.
Tripole, M.R. 1994. *Faith Beyond Justice.* St. Louis, MO: The Institute of Jesuit Sources.
Vance, R., and Colella, A. 1990. "Effects of Two Types of Feedback on Goal Acceptance and Personal Goals," *Journal of Applied Psychology, 75*(1990), 68–76.
Vroom, V.H., and Yetton, P.W. 1973. *Leadership and Decision-making.* Pittsburgh: University of Pittsburgh Press is the original version; Vroom, V.H., and Jago, E.J. 1988. *The New Leadership: Managing Participation in Organizations.* Englewood Cliffs, NJ: Prentice-Hall, is the most recent version.
Williams, S. 2018. "Developing the Capacity of Culturally Competent Leaders to Redress Inequitable Outcomes: Increasing Opportunities for Historically Marginalized Students," *Administrative Issues Journal: Education, Practice and Research, 8*(1), 48–58.
Zuker, R.E. 1983. *Mastering Assertiveness Skills.* New York: AMACOM.

Index

A, B, Cs, of strategic planning, 93–94
accommodation, in management of conflict, 68, 70
active listening, 46, 49–50
aggressive communication, 49
arbitration, 84–85
assertive communication style, 46, 48–49
attitudes, 10–12, 16, 18
attribution, 10, 13–14
avoidance, 68–69

behavioral view of leadership, 22
bias, implicit and explicit, 11, 12, 16
Blanchard, R., 31, 36–37, 89
Bolman, L., 22–25
brainstorming, 61
Bryson, J., 93–94

career ladder, 42–43
case study approach, 2
change, integrated approach, 99–101
change agent, 94, 99, 102, 104–5, 107–8
collaboration in conflict management, 70–71
collaboration in negotiation, 80
collaborative strategic planning, 93–96
collective bargaining, 81–83, 85–86

communication, 45
communication process, 45
compromise, in management conflict, 68–70
conflict resolution, 69
contingency theory, 6–7
contract administration, 85
control theory, 40
covenants, 106
cultural competency, 16–17

Deal, T., 22–25
decision making, 55
Delphi technique, 61–64
Depree, M., 113
diagnostic approach, 13, 131
Dweck, C., 35

empowerment, 75
ethical decision making, 57–58

feedback, value of, 50
force-field analysis, 103–4
forcing, 68, 70

Glasser, W., 38, 40
goal-setting theory, 41
Goldaber, I., 81–82
grievance procedures, 83, 85–86

group decision making, 58
group dynamic, 59
groupthink, 59–60
growth mindset, 35–36

halo effect, 11–12
heart, 113. *See also* trust and respect
Hersey, P., 26–27

Instructional leadership model, 29–30
interpersonal relations, 90, 106

Johari window, 47–48

leadership, 21
leadership frames, 121
learning process:
   behaviorist approach, 14
   cognitive approach, 15
   social approach, 15–16

Lewin, 104
locus of control, 14

Maslow's theory, 38–40
matrix design, 51–52
mediation, 84–85
mission-centric leadership, 29
motivation, 35

need theories, 38–40
negotiations, 75, 79
nominal group technique, 61–62
nonassertive communication, 48–49

open system theory, 4–6
organizational culture, 14
organizational structure, 3

perception, 11
perceptual distortions, 11
planning, comprehensive and strategic, 91
planning process, 91, 95
planning task force (PTF), 94–95
power, 75
power, sources of, 77
projection, 11–12

redesign of work, 41–42
reinforcement theory, 37
reward systems, 18, 37

Sanaghan, P., 93–96
self-fulfilling prophecy, 11–13
servant leadership, 24, 118
Simon, H., 59, 105
situational leadership, 22
social systems theory, 3–4, 52
sources or power, 77
   legitimate power, 77
   organizational, 77–78
   personal power, 78–79
   position power, 77
   reward power, 77
stereotyping, 11
strategic planning, 89
systems theory, 3–4

trait perspective, 21
transformational leadership, 28–29
trust and respect, 116

vision, educational, 30–31
Vroom-Yetton model, 53–54, 56–57

win-win negotiations, 79–81
work redesign, 41–42

About the Authors

Chris Heasley is an assistant professor of educational leadership in the School of Health Studies and Education at Saint Joseph's University, Philadelphia. Before teaching, he served more than eighteen years as a university administrator at both public and private institutions of higher education. He teaches courses on advanced quantitative research in education; educational leaders as researcher and reflective practitioner; and policy, politics, and community relations.

Robert Palestini has been an educator for more than fifty years, serving as a high school science teacher, principal, superintendent of schools, and university dean. He is currently dean emeritus and professor of educational leadership, as well as the founding executive director of the Educational Leadership Institute and Center for Catholic Urban Education at Saint Joseph's University.

www.ingramcontent.com/pod-product-compliance
Lightning Source LLC
Chambersburg PA
CBHW022015300426
44117CB00005B/200